THE
SHAPE OF
THINGS

Neil LaBute

BROADWAY PLAY PUBLISHING INC
224 E 62nd St, NY NY 10065-8201
212 772-8334 fax: 212 772-8358
http://www.BroadwayPlayPubl.com

First printing: October 2003
Second printing: September 2004
This printing: September 2011
I S B N: 978-0-88145-222-8

Book design: Marie Donovan
Word processing: Microsoft Word for Windows
Typographic controls: Xerox Ventura Publisher 2.0 P E
Typeface: Palatino
Printed on recycled acid-free paper and bound in the U S A

THE SHAPE OF THINGS premiered in London at the Almeida Theatre on 24 May 2001. It was subsequently produced in New York at the Promenade Theater.

CHARACTERS & SETTING

ADAM
EVELYN
JENNY
PHILLIP

a liberal arts college in a conservative midwestern town

AUTHOR'S NOTE

the / in certain lines denotes an attempt at interruption
or overlap by a given character

(The museum. Silence. Darkness)

(Large white box of a room. Wooden floor polished to a high shine. Several hallways feed off in different directions.)

(A young woman stands near a stretch of velvet rope. She has a can in one hand and stares up at an enormous human sculpture. After a moment, a young man [in uniform] steps across the barrier and approaches her.)

ADAM: ...you stepped over the line. Miss./ Umm, you stepped over...

EVELYN: I know./It's "Ms".

ADAM: Okay, sorry, Ms, but, ahh...

EVELYN: I meant to./Step over...

ADAM: What?/Yeah, I figured you did. I mean, the way you did it and all, kinda deliberate like./You're not supposed to do that.

EVELYN: I know./That's why I tried it....

ADAM: Why?

EVELYN: ...to see what would happen.

ADAM: Oh. Well...me, I s'pose.

EVELYN: "Me?"

ADAM: No, I mean, I'm what happens, I guess. I have to walk over, like I've done, and ask you to take a step back. Could you, please?/Step back?

EVELYN: And if someone doesn't?/What then?

ADAM: ...you're not gonna step back?

EVELYN: No...I mean, yes, I probably will, but just for interest's sake, what would you do if?

ADAM: I'm...geez, I'm not sure. I've never had anyone not step back. I've only said it, like, four times. And every time they've done it. Stepped back.

EVELYN: What if I'm your first? Non-stepper, I mean. Then what?

ADAM: Hell, I dunno...I'm off in, like, ten minutes, I'd probably just stand here, make sure you didn't touch anything.

EVELYN: Really?

ADAM: Pretty much, yeah. I'd let next shift talk to you, kick you out or whatever.

EVELYN: You wouldn't grab me or anything?

ADAM: Nah. That's too...you know. That's a total hassle, you end up rolling around on the ground, you'd probably sue the place, or me, and then...I'd get fired for doing my job. Screw that... *(Beat)* Could you do that for me, though?

EVELYN: Which, roll around on the ground or sue you?

ADAM: No, step back behind the line there...
I'd appreciate it.

EVELYN: Not really.

ADAM: No, seriously, I would. I'd definitely appreciate it....

EVELYN: I mean, "not really" I'm not going to....

ADAM: I thought you just said you probably will....

EVELYN: Yeah, "probably." I decided not to.

ADAM: Hey, you're not gonna mess up my weekend with this, are you?

EVELYN: I wasn't planning on it, but...I'm not completely against it, either.

ADAM: See, if you get all crazy, then I gotta write up a report and stuff, I'm here till six, six-thirty easy, and I have a second job to get to.

EVELYN: Tonight? *Friday* night?

ADAM: Yep. Right after this, at the video store...

EVELYN: Why would anyone work two jobs on Friday night?

ADAM: ...for money.

EVELYN: Of course...sorry. *(Looks at him again)* Oh...oh, right! That's where I...I've seen you in there. You helped me once, I think.

ADAM: Yeah?/With what?

EVELYN: Uh-huh./*The Picture of Dorian Gray*...you found it in Drama, not Classics./Somebody'd misplaced it....

ADAM: Right, I remember that./Yes...behind *Cabaret*. The "Joel Grey" fiasco...

EVELYN: Yeah, you said you found it with *Dirty Dancing* once, too, or something....

ADAM: I did, you're right...that's funny.

EVELYN: Anyway, you helped me, that was nice....

ADAM: Thanks. But, you're not gonna return the favor, right?

EVELYN: You mean the...? *(She points back toward the velvet rope.)*

ADAM: Yeah.

EVELYN: No, sorry, I can't.

ADAM: Why is that? *(Pointing)* It's a pretty good-sized sculpture. You can see it just fine from there....

EVELYN: Truthfully? I'm building up my nerve, and if
I go back over, I'll probably be a big wuss about it and
take off....

ADAM: About what? The "wuss" part, I mean....

EVELYN: I was going to deface the statue.

ADAM: Oh. Oh... *(Pointing)* Is that paint?

EVELYN: Yes.

ADAM: Great...from across the room, I thought you
were maybe one of the cleaning people, I was hoping
that was Lemon Pledge or something....

(They share a smile.)

ADAM: Paint's not really the best thing to have in a
museum. People'll definitely take that the wrong way....

EVELYN: How do they know which way to take it?

ADAM: I'm thinking outside would be the general
direction they'd steer you with spray paint...
why do you have that?

EVELYN: I was going to do something to the nude.
Mess it up or...

ADAM: What, you mean, like, colour it or something?

EVELYN: I was thinking more of painting a big dick on
it, but whatever....

ADAM: Well, you could still colour it in...the dick.

(EVELYN *smiles at this.*)

EVELYN: True. It might look kinda weird....

ADAM: Oh, I think a graffiti penis is gonna be plenty
odd already.... *(Beat)* So, right over the leaves there,
or just a free-floating number?

EVELYN: Probably anatomically correct. I mean,
if you're gonna do it, why not....

ADAM: ...do it right? Absolutely. And, would "why" be completely out of the question here?

EVELYN: Why the "dick"?

ADAM: Uh-huh. I mean, since I basically have to jump you now if you lift that can up, it'd help with my report....

EVELYN: Because I don't like art that isn't true.

ADAM: "True." What do you mean?

EVELYN: False art. I hate that....

(Other patrons drift past. They watch them go.)

ADAM: No, I understand the words you've used here, although they're both pretty subjective: "art." "Truth."

EVELYN: Exactly! That's the beauty of art...it's subjective.

ADAM: Right, but see, I don't know what you're referring to then. I mean, specifically.... *(Beat)* Didn't Oscar Wilde say something like, "In art there is no such thing as a universal truth..." Or whatever?

EVELYN: Yes...very good. "A truth in art is that whose contradictory is also true." Right, but that's an *aesthetic*. I'm talking about practicalities. Censorship. *(She points.)* This sculpture. It's fake, it's not real. Therefore, false art...

ADAM: No, it's a Fornecelli, it definitely is. I read the little thingie there one time....

EVELYN: Yes, but the leaf cluster isn't.

ADAM: It's not?/What is it, a pastie or something, like strippers have?

EVELYN: No./It's plaster...it was added by a committee who had complaints from local townspeople./Uh-huh./ They made a petition and got that put on, thereby removing its subjectivity as art.

ADAM: Really?/I didn't know that.../When did they do this?

EVELYN: Seven or eight years ago now, I think. Before I got here, anyway./See, they objected to his "thing." The shape of it. Said it was too *life-like*. *(Beat)* It's supposed to be "god," you know...that's what pisses 'em off.

ADAM: Huh./Yeah...he's not really supposed to have one of those, is he?

EVELYN: No, and I don't know why...we're always calling him "the creator." *(Beat)* Look at it, you can see the...see right behind the grapes there, you can just see his....

ADAM: ...grapes. Yes. You're absolutely, huh. Didn't even cover him properly. Shoddy craftmanship!

EVELYN: I mean, if you're gonna do it, at least....

ADAM: ...exactly. Do it right. *(Beat)* But why deface the thing? I mean, just out of curiosity. Why not, say, knock the plaster off and expose his...you know...cluster... if you're trying to....

EVELYN: Because. That's so...expected.

ADAM: Ahh...so, you're a student, then, or is this just basic anarchy?

EVELYN: Yep. Student.

ADAM: Me too.

EVELYN: Yeah? What's your emphasis?

ADAM: Ummm...taking out school loans, primarily, but I do sit in on a few English classes. You're in art?

EVELYN: Mmmm-hmmm. M F A./Applied theory and crit...

ADAM: Oh./So, is this, like, a project?

EVELYN: No, I'm just getting started on my thesis project now. A big sorta installation..."thingie."

ADAM: That's a good word, huh? "Thingie."

EVELYN: It is.... *(Points)* Anyway, *this* is only a pet peeve....

ADAM: Thesis? You're graduating....

EVELYN: In May.

ADAM: 'Kay. I'm only a Junior....

EVELYN: Huh. You seem older.

ADAM: Well, I am. I mean, older than twenty, anyhow...I worked for a couple years. Made money.

EVELYN: Not enough, though. Still got two jobs...

ADAM: Don't forget the school loans...

EVELYN: Right. So, basically, you're...fucked.

ADAM: Yep. But at least I'm educated, so I *comprehend* that I'm fucked....

(They stand there for a moment. ADAM checks his watch; EVELYN shakes her spray can.)

EVELYN: You're cute. I don't like the way you wear your hair....

ADAM: Thank you. I think....

EVELYN: No, you're definitely cute, but you shouldn't style it so much. Your hair. Just let it go...

ADAM: 'kay. I'll try that....

EVELYN: Your relief's late.

ADAM: Yeah. Typical...

EVELYN: So, do you have to stay at your station until they spell you, or...?

ADAM: No, at punch-out time, I'm supposed to get down there and do it. They can really be pricks about that....

EVELYN: You should go then....

ADAM: Right. Yeah, I...can I call you?

EVELYN: What do you wanna call me?

ADAM: Up. Just up, right now. Talk, maybe get crazy, take you to dinner...

EVELYN: Okay. Ahh...sure. *(Beat)* Do they allow you to do that here?

ADAM: What, eat dinner?

EVELYN: I meant hit on the patrons....

ADAM: ...ummm, no, they've got a pretty strict policy about that, too, actually. But...

EVELYN: ...ahh, the great equalizer. "But."

ADAM: Exactly. I'll take the risk....

EVELYN: ...good answer, grasshopper.

ADAM: Huh?

EVELYN: "Kung Fu." On TV. Remember when he was a kid? The old guy with the fakey contact lenses, and the....

ADAM: Oh, right...sure. "Grasshopper." I don't really watch much television....

EVELYN: My brothers loved that show. *(Beat)* So, do you want a number?

ADAM: Absolutely! *(Checks)* Damn, I don't have a pen.

EVELYN: Me either. *(Thinks)* Here...gimme the jacket.

ADAM: What?

EVELYN: Your jacket. Take it off for a second.

ADAM: Oh, that's, umm...it's supposed to be a "blazer."

EVELYN: What?

ADAM: It's my own...'s not part of the uniform. It's mine.

EVELYN: Good. Then you'll always have it on you... from the looks of it.

(ADAM *follows her orders.* EVELYN *lays the coat open on the floor, looks around, then uncaps the paint and sprays a phone number inside.*)

EVELYN: ...don't worry, it dries quick.

ADAM: Thanks. Okay, so, I'll...yeah. (*He glances back.*) Good luck with the...nice to meet you. Again.

EVELYN: You too.

(ADAM *smiles at her, looks back again, walks off.* EVELYN *is left alone. She turns back to the statue and starts shaking her paint can. The little ball bearings inside rattle loudly.*)

(The auditorium patio)

(Faux-Greek building with a Spanish roof. Banners proclaim "Mercy College". Theater posters behind glass.)

(ADAM standing with EVELYN. He looks a bit different, not as bulky and he's letting his hair go. Same jacket under his arm.)

EVELYN: ...no, seriously. You have.

ADAM: Yeah?

EVELYN: No question.

ADAM: I dunno. I think I still look....

EVELYN: You can definitely tell. You can.

ADAM: Really?

EVELYN: Definitely. Plus, the hair.../I bet your friends say something. Twenty bucks...

ADAM: Well, I'm glad..../I mean, I can't tell and so I figured...twenty bucks?

EVELYN: Yes. That's because you see "you" every day. Shower, getting dressed, that kind of thing. But...

ADAM: So do you.

EVELYN: I don't see you shower. Or getting dressed...

ADAM: No, I meant every day. So far, anyway, since we first went to....

EVELYN: I know, I'm kidding.

ADAM: Oh. Okay... *(Beat)* I'd like that, though. If you would....

EVELYN: Which?

ADAM: Both if you want. Either. Anything, any moment I can get with you...that's what I'd like.

EVELYN: Ask and you shall receive....

ADAM: So, I'm asking, then.

EVELYN: So you shall be receiving then....

(They share a brief kiss; he looks around self-consciously.)

ADAM: P D A. Public display of affection. I'm not used to that....

EVELYN: No? I don't mind....

ADAM: Really?

EVELYN: Nah, whose business is it? Ours, right? Kiss if we want to, make love in a bathroom stall...who cares?

ADAM: I'd start with the administration....

EVELYN: Yeah, but why should they? I mean...we're two adults, we....

ADAM: I think this is a bigger discussion than before Jenny and Phillip get here..../I mean, no, I'd love to have it with you, the discussion, and I agree, somewhat, but....

EVELYN: Whatever./I understand....

ADAM: Another time, we'll definitely discuss it.

EVELYN: Another time...I'd rather do it.

ADAM: Lemme go check the men's room... *(He laughs.)* ...you amaze me.

EVELYN: I'm glad. *(Beat)* And you amaze *me*, you do. Look at you!

ADAM: ...it's just a little jogging.

EVELYN: No, it's not. It's not just that...you're running, you're eating better, are you still lifting?

ADAM: Yeah...I mean, I didn't today, but....

EVELYN: That's okay.

ADAM: No, I'm gonna...so, yeah, alright, it's a whole routine thing. You're right....

EVELYN: Do you like doing it?

ADAM: Honestly...no. I totally hate it!

(They laugh.)

EVELYN: So why would you...?

ADAM: Because you suggested it. Which is kinda pathetic, but true....

EVELYN: You shouldn't do something you don't wanna do.

ADAM: Yeah, you should, why not? If it's for someone...I mean, I'm doing it for you.

EVELYN: It's a life change. Really...

ADAM: Right.

EVELYN: I gave you a couple ideas and you're changing your entire life. I'm very proud of you.

ADAM: Thank you... *(Cockney)* ...'enry 'iggins.

EVELYN: What's that?/Who's....

ADAM: Nothing./'S from a book. Play, actually.

EVELYN: Oh. Not the one we're seeing, though, is it?

ADAM: No, no, a musical...this is, umm, Medea.

EVELYN: Oh yeah, right. *(Smiles)* I read this as an undergrad, I *like* it....

ADAM: Ahh, you like Medea, huh? Should I be nervous?

EVELYN: No, not too much...I mean, unless we have kids.

ADAM: *(Laughing)* ...alright...

EVELYN: So...are you still keeping your journal? It really does help....

ADAM: Yes.

EVELYN: Will you let me read it?

ADAM: ...some time.

EVELYN: Good.

(They stand for a moment. EVELYN *checks her watch.)*

ADAM: And what about you?

EVELYN: What about me?

ADAM: That's what I mean...I don't know.

EVELYN: What?

ADAM: Nothing. I don't really know anything about you....

EVELYN: Yes, you do!

ADAM: I don't. Not really...

EVELYN: What's my name?

ADAM: Evelyn.

EVELYN: Where am I from?

ADAM: Illinois. Near Chicago?

EVELYN: Yes. How old am I?

ADAM: Ummm...twenty-five, maybe.

EVELYN: That's exactly right. Almost twenty-six. Sign?

ADAM: Gemini, I think....

EVELYN: The twins, yes.

ADAM: Does that mean you have a split personality?

EVELYN: No, it means I was born in June.

ADAM: Oh. *(Beat)* And you're, what, a sculptress, right? An artist...

EVELYN: Yep. Anything else you wanna know?

ADAM: Yes...everything!

EVELYN: So ask then...

ADAM: Well...why are you always asking me questions if it's no big deal.

EVELYN: Because you make me curious...I'm a curious person.

ADAM: I'm curious, too, though!

EVELYN: Like I said...so ask then.

ADAM: ...why do you like me?

EVELYN: What?

ADAM: Me...why would you like me? I'm not anything, I mean...and you're so....

EVELYN: Don't do that, okay? That's the only thing about you I don't like...what you see in yourself. Or don't see. Your insecurities. *(Beat)* Do you like me?

ADAM: Of course, you know I do....

EVELYN: Do I appear to like you? Hmm?

ADAM: Yes...it seems like it, yeah.

EVELYN: I do like you. Do you think I'm smart?

ADAM: I think you're amazing...and you have a *great* ass. Just thought you should know....

EVELYN: Not part of my query, but thank you.

ADAM: Welcome...

EVELYN: And do I seem to know my own mind? I mean, generally....

ADAM: No question.

EVELYN: So, don't you trust me, then, to know how I feel?

ADAM: Yeah. No, you're right....

EVELYN: Don't worry about *why* when *what* is right in front of you.

ADAM: Those're very wise words from someone with such a great ass....

EVELYN: *(Playfully)* Kiss me, grasshopper...

(They start to kiss again as A young couple approaches.)

JENNY: Ah, ah, ah...P D A.

PHILLIP: I don't think anybody wants to watch you kiss, Adam...we'll be eating later.

ADAM: Hey, Phillip, hello! Evelyn, this is Phillip, and his fiancée, Jenny....

("Hellos" all around.)

PHILLIP: So, we should grab our tickets, and.... *(Stopping to look)* Adam, what's up with you? D'you lost weight?

ADAM: ...a little, maybe.

JENNY: No, he cut his hair...or something. That's it, right?

ADAM: Umm, yeah. I mean, both, sort of.

PHILLIP: Huh. Okay, so, let's...come on.

(JENNY and PHILLIP lead the way. EVELYN stares at ADAM as they follow; he pulls a twenty out of his pocket and places it in her hand.)

(The living room)

(Fairly nice digs for a student, with matching furniture and lamps. Forest mural covers one wall.)

*(*ADAM *and* EVELYN *sitting on a couch.* JENNY *and* PHILLIP *in opposing chairs. Everyone holds a drink.)*

ADAM: ...so, tell me this again, you're going to what?

PHILLIP: Underwater. We're going to get married underwater....

ADAM: You've gotta be kidding me!

PHILLIP: ...like those *Life* magazine photos you see or whatever./Seriously.

EVELYN: Huh./Is that, like, a "California" thing?

JENNY: No. We wanted to try something bold....

EVELYN: That oughta do it.

ADAM: This is crazy, really. And, so, if we want to attend we have to....

PHILLIP: ...get in the tank with us. You bet.

JENNY: No, honey, I thought we said....

PHILLIP: ...we haven't, okay, no, we haven't settled that part completely, but....

JENNY: My dad could never do that. I mean, my mom would try, she would, but dad....

PHILLIP: Maybe people can watch from the glass window things or whatever, but I'd prefer if they came in with us.... *(He drains his glass, looking at* ADAM*)*

ADAM: That is nuts....

EVELYN: Well, I applaud you. I think it's very....

PHILLIP: *(To* EVELYN*)* Yeah, well, don't expect my
buddy here to follow in our footsteps. He's the least
adventurous person I know....

EVELYN: Really?

PHILLIP: Absolutely! And the marriage thing? Uh-uh,
not gonna happen, sorry. I don't know how many
nights I listened to this guy say, "not me, man,
I'm never getting hooked, no way, man..."

EVELYN: Is that right? Well, well...

ADAM: Listen, don't encourage him. My room-mate
doesn't need any....

PHILLIP: ...former room-mate...

ADAM: ...more encouragement. *(Beat)* I'm gonna look
stupid in one of those wet suits.

PHILLIP: Hey, let's not be a party-pooper here, my
friend... *(Indicating* JENNY*)* ...this could've been yours.

*(*ADAM *laughs thinly;* EVELYN *doesn't understand.)*

ADAM: I know, I know....

PHILLIP: Right?

EVELYN: I'm lost. What's...?

PHILLIP: I stole Jenny away from Adam....

ADAM: Come on...

PHILLIP: I did! *(To* JENNY*)* Didn't I?

JENNY: No, you didn't, stop being.... *(To* EVELYN*)*
Adam and I had a class together, but he never got
up the nerve to ask me out.

EVELYN: Is that true?

ADAM: Something like that...

JENNY: Four months we sat next to each other—
I'm borrowing his pen, like, all the time, hint-hint—
and he's this total monk the whole semester...anyway,
Phil picks him up from class one day, sees me, and we
went to mini-golf that same night.

PHILLIP: I cannot tell a lie...I've got the moves, God help
me.

ADAM: God help all of us....

(A collective laugh)

EVELYN: Well, like I said, I think it's great. It's really
amazing, it is, to find anybody willing to take a risk
today. To look a little silly or different or anything.
Bravo! *(Toasts)* To people with balls...

(They all toast, even PHILLIP *with his empty glass,
but he looks over at* ADAM. ADAM *blushes.*

PHILLIP: "Balls," huh? Yep, that's my Jenny....

*(*JENNY *slaps him on the shoulder and blushes again.)*

EVELYN: You know what I mean. Guts. That kinda
thing...

JENNY: Right. I got it.

PHILLIP: *(Toasting)* "To balls, long may they wave..."

(They all smile and "mock" drink again.)

PHILLIP: I'll tell you what took some balls, the museum
thing, a few weeks back, with the...balls. You guys read
about that?! I mean, Adam, of course you did, you were
supposed to be *guarding* it, but—Evelyn, you hear about
it?

JENNY: *(Whispering)* The penis...

EVELYN: *(Whispering)* Yes, I did. Why are we
whispering?

PHILLIP: Because you don't say "penis" in Jenny's
house. But we're at my place now, and so we sing
it from the eaves! "Penis!! Pe-nis!!!"

ADAM: Okay, bar's closing, last call....

PHILLIP: No, seriously, do you believe that shit?
Somebody with the gall to do that kinda bullshit
on our campus?! That fucking burns me up....

EVELYN: I'm an artist, so I didn't....

ADAM: We should probably get, ummm....

PHILLIP: I mean, this isn't Berkeley! *(Beat)* What does
that mean, anyway? "I'm an artist?"

EVELYN: It means nothing, really, just that I understand
the impulse....

PHILLIP: You what?!

ADAM: Evelyn, maybe we should....

PHILLIP: No, wait Adam, I wanna hear...
what "impulse?" It's called "vandalism."

JENNY: Does anyone want dessert?

*(PHILLIP holds up a hand to hush the group. He turns back to
EVELYN.)*

PHILLIP: No, hold on, this is rich. Go ahead...

EVELYN: Just that...I don't think it was just kids playing.
I think it was a sort of statement, a kind of....

PHILLIP: ...a statement?

EVELYN: Yeah, I do....

JENNY: What kind of statement would that be? It was
pornography....

EVELYN: No, it wasn't.

JENNY: Yes, it was....

EVELYN: Pornography is meant to titillate, to excite you. Did you see a picture of what happened?

PHILLIP: We did, yeah....

EVELYN: Does a penis excite you? I mean, just any ol' penis?

PHILLIP: You're funny. And that's not the point.

EVELYN: It's totally the point...how about you, Jenny, did you like what you saw? Did it get you hot?

PHILLIP: This is, like, uncalled for, okay? All she said was....

EVELYN: I know what she said, why don't you let her speak? *(To* JENNY*)* Did you wanna see anything else? Huh? Okay, then...all I'm saying is that, in my *opinion*, it wasn't pornography, it was a statement. Of course, that's the beauty of statements, like art, they're subjective. You and I can think completely different things and we can both be right...unless, and this seems quite probable, you just can't stand to lose an argument.

(Quiet for a moment from the group.)

PHILLIP: Wow. The postgraduate mind at work...

ADAM: I'll help you get dessert, Jenny, if you want to....

JENNY: ...I still don't think that makes it a statement. It's graffiti....

EVELYN: What do you mean, it would be a huge statement...especially for a town like this.

PHILLIP: Hey, some of us are from "a town like this," so maybe you should watch it.

EVELYN: Well, we've all gotta be from somewhere....

PHILLIP: What do you mean by that?

EVELYN: I mean, it's a little college town in the middle of nowhere and....

PHILLIP: One you chose, presumably....

EVELYN: No, it chose me, actually. *Full* scholarship.
So, as I was saying....

PHILLIP: You've got a real winning way, you know that?

ADAM: Look, Phil, it's no big deal, let's just....

PHILLIP: Which "take back the night" rally did you find
her at, Adam?

EVELYN: ...can I finish, please?! Jesus, you're really the
obnoxious type, you know that? *(To* ADAM*)* How long
did you have to stomach this guy?

(Everyone except EVELYN *sort of freezes on that one.)*

ADAM: Evelyn.

EVELYN: Anyhow, who knows what the person was
saying by it, we don't, but I think it was a gesture.
A kind of manifesto, if you will....

PHILLIP: *(Dryly)* I don't think a person's dick can be a
manifesto. Uh-uh. You can write a manifesto on your
thing, but your thing can't be one...I'm sure I read that
somewhere.

EVELYN: See? You're just trying to be....

PHILLIP: I'm not trying to be anything! Who the hell do
you think you are, a few double dates and telling me
anything about who I am? Un-fucking-believable!

JENNY: This is getting a little, ahh....

PHILLIP: ...Adam, you can really pick 'em. Wow, man!

ADAM: Look, it's not, let's just forget the....

EVELYN: You're not gonna take his side in this, are you?

ADAM: I'm not taking sides, I'm trying to get outta here
with just a touch of dignity, okay? Jesus...

JENNY: I've got a test tomorrow, anyway....

PHILLIP: "Statement," she says!

EVELYN: Shut the fuck up, alright? Just fuck right off...how would you know? I think she was making one, so that's my opinion....

ADAM: Jenny, thanks for everything. Phillip, I'll call ya, or whatever, but we're gonna....

PHILLIP: Yeah? How do you know it was a girl?

EVELYN: ...I don't. I didn't say it was a woman.

PHILLIP: Girl, woman, whatever. You said "she," how do you know that?

EVELYN: I don't, I just said. It's a guess. What it was, where it was placed. An *educated* guess...

PHILLIP: You are not...she's not trying to take a poke at my being an undergrad, is she? Adam, tell me she didn't just....

JENNY: Can we stop, now, please?! You guys...

ADAM: Evelyn, let's go...

PHILLIP: Hey, artiste...how'd you know it was a woman who painted the cock, huh? Very, very suspicious there...

EVELYN: You are such a prick, man, how do you go on, day after day? (*To* ADAM) Let's go... (*She rises, snatches up her things and moves towards the door*) Adam? Are you coming?

ADAM: I'm...yeah, but, just go. I'll meet you downstairs, I just wanna...go ahead.

EVELYN: 'kay. (*To* JENNY) You're very sweet. Good luck... (*She heads for the door and exits.*)

PHILLIP: "Good luck." Hey, fuck you! (*To* ADAM) Where in hell did you meet that bitch?!/What'd she do, give you a haircut and a blow job and now you're her puppy?!!/You don't have to go....

ADAM: ...at the museum./No, I'm not her.... *(To* JENNY*)* The wedding sounds great. Really...it sounds...yeah.

(He wanders off. PHILLIP *and* JENNY *sit in silence.)*

PHILLIP: ...what?

(The bedroom)

(An explosion of color and patterns. An enormous bed in the middle of it all. Groovy lighting.)

(ADAM and EVELYN in bed. Holding each other, staring off. A video camera on a tripod nearby)

EVELYN: ...umm, nice.

ADAM: Very. Yes.

EVELYN: Our bodies are beginning to understand one another....

ADAM: You're right, I mean....

EVELYN: Getting a rhythm. And less inhibited.

ADAM: Yep.

(He leans over and whispers something in her ear. A huge smile across her face. She turns and whispers back to him. They laugh and kiss for a moment. They hold one another.)

EVELYN: *(Quietly)* Were you always like this before? So...you know....

ADAM: ...shy? Just about the fact that no one would sleep with me. That's all.

EVELYN: Come on...

ADAM: Seriously. You're only, like, I dunno, the third person I've ever....

EVELYN: ...no...

ADAM: Yes, I mean it. And they were both young. I mean, I was too, I wasn't, like, hanging out at a *day care*

or anything, but...it was during high school mostly.
So...you're sort of in uncharted waters here.

EVELYN: I don't wanna blow your cover but...
I could kinda tell.

ADAM: *(Smiling)* Yeah? Well, that's okay....

EVELYN: And nobody here at school?

ADAM: Nothing serious. Dates. Some close calls.
But not anyone...you know.

EVELYN: ...like Jenny.

ADAM: No.

EVELYN: You sorry you didn't ask her out? I mean,
if I wasn't in the equation....

ADAM: Not really. We just never got the right...
whatever. I sorta blew that one. Anyway, it's kind
of weird talking about....

EVELYN: It's okay. That's nice to see, every so often.
Someone gallant...

ADAM: Which is medieval for "loser"... *(Beat)* I wanna
tell you something—and this is not because we've been
sleeping together or because you mentioned another
girl, it's not—I can't stop thinking about you. I can't.
I mean, it's not like a stalker situation...yet...but I'm
finding myself hanging out by your classes. Following
you...

EVELYN: I've noticed....

ADAM: I figured, yeah. And taking my jacket off,
like, thirty times a day and looking at your number.
Staring at it. Wondering if you're looking at my
number. And writing your name on anything!
All over my books. In my *food*. Seriously, tracing
your name in whatever I'm eating. I'm so whipped...
you are dangerously close to owning me.

EVELYN: Wow...

ADAM: I just signed my relationship death warrant, didn't I?/What a dork...

EVELYN: ...no, it's sweet!/It is!! *(She kisses him.)* So...did you enjoy tonight?

ADAM: Uh-huh, dinner was great. Trip into the city...that was fun. I like your car....

EVELYN: I *meant* the performance.

ADAM: Oh, right, *that*. Umm, yeah, you know, it was, uhh...not really.

(EVELYN studies him, seems disappointed.)

EVELYN: ...that's alright. "S fine.

ADAM: No, it's not that I didn't *enjoy* it, it was okay....

EVELYN: You didn't, though, did you?

ADAM: I mean, you know...sort of....

EVELYN: No, I don't know. I don't "sort of" enjoy Art. I either like it or I don't. It's not a *casserole*....

ADAM: I know that, come on!...

EVELYN: Art is visceral! You're supposed to experience the thing, feel it....

ADAM: So, I guess I didn't "feel it", then. Forgive me...

EVELYN: Okay, sorry, that was...I just hate that kind of "middle of the road" crap response to something. "It was interesting. And different." God, that's so West Coast!

ADAM: Hey, it's just an *opinion*....

EVELYN: That's fine, no, of course, I don't mean that you can't have an opinion....

ADAM: ...thank you...

EVELYN: ...I just wish it was right./Kidding!

ADAM: Geez.../You're funny.

EVELYN: Look, I was hoping you'd like it, that's all....

ADAM: Well, you can still hope....

EVELYN: Ha ha. *(Beat)* Anyhow, it's fine if our opinions differ. Love it, hate it, whatever. I just don't think you can dismiss that kind of conceptual creativity with a yawn and a "where should we eat?"

ADAM: I didn't *yawn*...my mouth was just hanging open.

EVELYN: You didn't think it was amazing?

ADAM: Yes, I did. I thought it was *amazing* that the cops didn't burst in and stop her....

EVELYN: Come on! How could you not find that moving, what she was doing?

ADAM: Easy...

EVELYN: Really?

ADAM: Yeah. I mean, granted, I usually love it when a woman removes her tampon in front of me...very sexy.

EVELYN: Uuuugh, Adam, don't say that! It's not meant to be *sexy*./Jesus, it's an expression of herself as an artist. As a woman. A *person*...

ADAM: I'm joking, you know that!/Okay, right, but the whole thing was....

EVELYN: It was so *incredible*...I couldn't believe what I was seeing!

ADAM: Me either.

EVELYN: See, I love her work. Her last show was fantastic....

ADAM: That's great, no, I'm just saying that it's hard for me to think of that as *Art*...what she was doing.

EVELYN: Why, because it's unconventional?

ADAM: No, because it's a Tampax.

EVELYN: You didn't get it, that's all....

ADAM: That's not true! That's...we just don't agree.
I wanted to like it....

EVELYN: Then why didn't you?

ADAM: I dunno. Maybe I'm narrow-minded, maybe
because I wasn't ready for it. Or *maybe* because she
was finger painting portraits of her daddy using her
menstrual blood....

EVELYN: She's completely influential...totally vanguard.

ADAM: I don't doubt it...I'm just saying that, to me,
it was nasty, it was private and I didn't feel like I was
supposed to be seeing that.

EVELYN: She allowed you to, though! She allowed you
into her work, her *world*...but in a highly theatrical way.

ADAM: Exactly my point! It's called "Theater," not
"Therapy."

EVELYN: No, it's called "Performance Art."

ADAM: It's called her "period!"

EVELYN: It's called "Your taste up your ass!"

(*They stop, staring at one another.*)

ADAM: ...did we just have our first fight?

EVELYN: I think so...yeah, we did. Cool. (*Smiles*)
Better mark it down in our diaries...

ADAM: Yep.

EVELYN: Hey, that's okay, we can do that, fight,
it's good.

ADAM: Why good?

EVELYN: ..."cause now we get to *make up*.... *(She crawls over to him, covering him in kisses. After a moment, she points at the video camera at the foot of the bed.)* Were you nervous earlier? I mean, about us with the video?

ADAM: Nah. Not really. *(Beat)* A bit...

EVELYN: Sure?

ADAM: Yeah. It's just...let's not watch it, okay? Do we have to do that?

EVELYN: Not if you don't want to....

ADAM: Good. I don't think I could get into that, actually....

EVELYN: Why not? It'd be fun....

ADAM: I don't really need to see myself doing that. Doing...stuff.

EVELYN: See, I'm totally different. I think everyone should see themselves doing it, and their friends should see it, too.

ADAM: And that's why the tape's gonna stay at my place....

(She smiles at this, kissing him.)

EVELYN: Don't be so frightened of everything.

ADAM: I'm not. Not frightened, anyway. I just don't think that's a thing other people need to see. Ever. My ass...

EVELYN: People like who...Phillip?

ADAM: No, that's fine, you can show it to him.... *(Beat)* Are you nuts?!

EVELYN: Why is he your friend?

ADAM: Do you really wanna go over that...?

EVELYN: I just don't get it.

ADAM: What's to get? We were room-mates, we occasionally see each other, have a drink....

EVELYN: I just don't think you need that kind of person in your life. No one does.

ADAM: *(Mock-serious)* ...it may be a touch early to start dictating who my friends are.

EVELYN: *(With charm)* Yeah...I s'pose.

ADAM: Geez, he really got under your skin, didn't he?

EVELYN: Under. Over. Around. I hate that kind of guy....

ADAM: What kind?

EVELYN: That kind. Whatever he is, that's what I hate....

ADAM: I'll let him know.

EVELYN: No, God, no, don't give him the satisfaction. And he'd take it, too, believe me....

ADAM: Nah, maybe it'd help him, you know, be better...or something.

EVELYN: The only thing that would help him is a fucking knife through his throat....

(They grow quiet for a moment. ADAM studies EVELYN.)

ADAM: Okay, I'm glad I don't have a pet rabbit or anything right now....

EVELYN: *(Laughing)* You know what I mean.

ADAM: Ummmm, no, not really.

EVELYN: I've just been around his type, that's all. And I don't like 'em.

ADAM: Yeah, I got that part....

EVELYN: No big deal.

ADAM: Right, no, it was the "knife through the throat" part that was the big deal, I thought....

EVELYN: Oh, that's just an expression.

ADAM: ...from where, Transylvania?

(She kisses him.)

EVELYN: No...from the "Scorned Girl's Handbook."

ADAM: Ahhh. Right...page 666.

EVELYN: *(Smiling)* You've been peeking. You know what happens to peekers, don't you?

ADAM: Well, if they're D Js, they usually get asked to play "Misty" on the radio all the time....

EVELYN: Close. No, I'll show you...but you have to do me a favor.

ADAM: What's that?

(She starts to slip under the covers.)

EVELYN: ...just smile. Smile into the camera. For as long as you can...

(The park)

(A series of large children's toys adrift in a patch of grass. Trees around the border. Clouds in the sky)

(JENNY waiting on a swing. Sitting by herself. After a moment, ADAM appears.)

ADAM: ...hey.

JENNY: Adam, hi, hello.

ADAM: Hi.

JENNY: Thanks for coming, I appreciate it.

ADAM: Of course, how's it going?

JENNY: You know...okay.

ADAM: Right.

JENNY: Lots to do for a wedding.

ADAM: I'll bet....

JENNY: Invitations to get out, arrangements to make....

ADAM: ...air tanks to fill....

(JENNY laughs lightly.)

JENNY: That too.

ADAM: So, you guys're still going through with that?

JENNY: That's what we're saying....

ADAM: What do you mean, "saying"?

JENNY: No, we are, it's what we're doing, I'm just....

ADAM: ...Jenny, what?

JENNY: I don't know. I'm, you know, worried.

ADAM: Why? About what?

JENNY: What do you think? Phillip. He's just...I dunno, being funny.

ADAM: Funny, how? Like "telling jokes" funny or "making letter bombs" funny?

JENNY: No, no bombs yet, but kind of...just funny. Odd. *(Beat)* Like, nice...

ADAM: "Nice?"

JENNY: Yeah, you know...sweet. Now, I love him and all, I do, you know that, but that's not the way I'd describe him to people. "Sweet." Would you?

(ADAM thinks for a moment.)

ADAM: No, I wouldn't exactly use his name and "sweet" in the same short story....

JENNY: And that's what's bugging me.

ADAM: Why, though? Maybe he's just....

JENNY: I've only seen him like this once before, maybe twice. Definitely once, when we were first going out and he was seeing somebody else, too. It was over, mostly, but he was still seeing her. Remember that?

ADAM: ...yeah. I do. The "other" one.

JENNY: The other Jenny, exactly. I'd call and I could hear him freeze up, stop for a moment if he answered and I said, "Hey, it's Jenny." He didn't know what to do, so he'd get all sort of sweet and fish around slowly until he figured out if it was her or me...God, I used to hate that!

ADAM: So, do you know anyone else named "Jenny" right now?

JENNY: No, I don't mean that, not the name so much as the feeling...that sense that there's someone else.

ADAM: Nah...

JENNY: Maybe I'm making it up, you know, my own insecurities and looking for a reason not to....

ADAM: *(Smiling)* ...dive in? Take the plunge? Jump off the deep end? Stop me before I...

JENNY: Cute...but yes. And that might be it, but I don't think so. I want to get married, I do, and I love the guy, whether he's sweet or not. It's just that I don't believe him now that he is....

ADAM: Well, you got me....

JENNY: Really? You don't know anything, haven't felt that or....

ADAM: I only see him, like, once a week in our survey course, so it's not like I'm in the inner circle any more....

JENNY: I know, I just thought that....

ADAM: ...but I would tell you, Jenny, I would, seriously.

JENNY: Really?

ADAM: I think so...I mean, that's a lousy thing to pass on to a person, and if I did, you know, know something and then told you, you'd more likely hate me forever than be grateful....

JENNY: Yeah, that's probably true....

ADAM: Ummmm, you could lie, you know, feel free.

JENNY: No, you're probably right....

ADAM: So, that doesn't exactly make me want to come clean here—which I don't have anything to come clean about, okay, honestly, I just mean, whatever—but I feel I would. I do, because I think you're pretty amazing, if the truth be known, and you're almost married so why shouldn't it be? The truth, I mean.

JENNY: ...thank you.

ADAM: Not a problem. Anyway, that's all I know. Which is, nothing....

JENNY: 'Kay. I'm just being stupid.

ADAM: Look, if you feel it, it's not stupid....

(JENNY *studies him hard.*)

JENNY: You're a lovely person, you know that?

ADAM: "Lovely?" Jesus, why don't you just call me "gay" and get it over with?

JENNY: Hey, "lovely" is nice...I wish there were a few more "lovely" people in the world. I mean it, you are. *(Looks at him again)* And getting cuter by the day. What is that girl doing to you?

ADAM: Lots...she's amazing, really.

JENNY: What happened to your...are you wearing...Adam, are those contacts?

ADAM: Yeah. Contacts.

JENNY: My God, this from the former "tape around the nose thing-y" champion....

ADAM: That was only for a week, that one time!

JENNY: Still, you've gotta admit....

ADAM: I do, it's amazing. I feel better....

JENNY: Better? You're, like, this totally hot guy now.... *(Beat)* I always thought you were handsome, anyway, but I didn't think you'd go in for the makeover thing.

ADAM: Me either. Who knew?

JENNY: Well, apparently she did.... *(Beat)* You are still seeing her, aren't you?

ADAM: Oh yeah. She's...you don't hold a grudge, all she said that night at your...God, I couldn't believe that!

JENNY: It was great. No, truthfully, it was, Phil needed to hear every word of that and he did, too. Hear it, I mean. Even said something after you guys left that night. Not an admittance of guilt, exactly, but as close to one as we're likely to hear from the guy....

ADAM: Really, what'd he say? I'm amazed....

JENNY: As was I...he put on quite the show....

ADAM: *(Sarcastically)* Yeah, I remember vaguely... they both did.

JENNY: Right, but later he said something like, "He could do worse."

ADAM: Not exactly a seal of approval...

JENNY: No, but a lot. For him. And after what she said....

ADAM: You're right. Huh.

JENNY: Hey...her middle name's not "Jenny" or anything, is it?

(ADAM *laughs at this.*)

ADAM: Nah, no such luck. It's "Ann." Evelyn Ann Thompson. Nice, right?

JENNY: Eat.

ADAM: Huh?

JENNY: "Eat." Those're her initials, the acronym of her names. E-a-t.

ADAM: Hey, that's cute....

JENNY: Oh God, you're a goner.

ADAM: I know, it's pathetic, isn't it?

JENNY: Yeah, somewhat...but lovely.

ADAM: Not that again...

(He puts a hand up to hide his face. JENNY grabs one of his hands, studying it.)

JENNY: What the heck is this? What is this?!

ADAM: What...?

JENNY: Did you stop biting your nails?

ADAM: Yeah, for, like, a month now...

JENNY: Don't tell me...

ADAM: It's true. She put some crap on them, slapped 'em out of my mouth a few times and that was it. I stopped....

JENNY: You have nails! This is crazy....

ADAM: It's no biggie....

JENNY: Ever since I've known you, three years now, your fingers've looked like raw meat...anyway, awful. And now you just quit?! This girl is the messiah.

ADAM: I've quit before....

JENNY: For, like, an hour! *(Beat)* I love this woman....

ADAM: Me too.

JENNY: Yeah, I see that. Wow... *(She looks over at ADAM again.)* And you'd really tell me if you knew something?

ADAM: ...I would. Yes.

JENNY: 'Kay. Damn, when did you get so cute?

(She kisses him lightly on the cheek. They look at each other for a long moment. Suddenly, they kiss. A real kiss, not a "great to see you, aren't we the best of friends" kiss. After a moment, they shudder to a halt.)

ADAM: ...shit.

JENNY: Yeah. Huh.

ADAM: What was that all about?

JENNY: I dunno. I just...I'm not sure.

ADAM: Look, I'm sorry.

JENNY: No, don't be. I am. I'm the one with the ring on....

ADAM: Yeah, good point. My friend's ring. Thanks for reminding me...

JENNY: Welcome.

ADAM: Oh, Gosh...dang it!

JENNY: ...no, listen. It wasn't because of, you know, my worries or whatever. How I feel about Phillip right now. It wasn't....

ADAM: Okay.

JENNY: It just...

ADAM: ...happened.

JENNY: Right. I've wanted to do that for a long time...three years....

ADAM: ...me too. *(Beat)* And now we take it down to the beach and bury it...don't we?

JENNY: Yeah. I mean, yes, definitely. I guess....

ADAM: Don't you think? We have to...Jesus, what're we even talking about?!

JENNY: No, we do. 'Course. Don't you want to?

ADAM: Bury it?

JENNY: Yes...or...

ADAM: No, we can't talk about...don't even say the... do you have a shovel in your car?

JENNY: I don't, no...but I have my car.

ADAM: ...my bike's right over there.

JENNY: Is it locked up?

ADAM: Uh-huh.

JENNY: Then it should be fine...if we were to go to the beach.

ADAM: I suppose so. It's a small town, after all.

JENNY: That's what people say....

ADAM: Good people. People we know and care about....

JENNY: Right. *(Beat)* Come on, we should go bury this. At the beach...

(They kiss again, then stand up slowly and walk off. She puts an arm through his.)

(The doctor's lounge)

(A glistening white room with relaxing colors schemes on the walls and furniture. End tables filled with magazines.)

*(*ADAM *and* EVELYN *sit on opposing couches, flipping through separate copies of* In Style. *After a moment,* ADAM *glances up and checks his watch.)*

ADAM: ...what time did they say?

EVELYN: Like, ten-thirty...

ADAM: And it's ten-fifty now....

EVELYN: No big deal, you always wait at the doctor's office.

ADAM: I know, I just have to be at work by twelve.

EVELYN: Today?

ADAM: Yeah, I told you that....

EVELYN: No, you didn't.

ADAM: I did...I always work Wednesdays.

EVELYN: Really?

ADAM: Yeah, every Wednesday.

EVELYN: Damn. I hope they....

ADAM: It's okay. I guess I could be a little late if I have to....

EVELYN: Sure?

ADAM: Uh-huh. It's alright...I mean, they hate it but I can make something up.

EVELYN: We can go.

ADAM: No, I wanna do this. I do.... *(Beat)* Who wouldn't want to get their nose chopped off?

EVELYN: Come on! It's not....

ADAM: I'm kidding. No, I think you're right about it....

EVELYN: It's just shaving it....

ADAM: Yeah, that's much better. "Shaving" your nose off...that settles the nerves.

EVELYN: You're only talking to them, anyway, that's all.

ADAM: I know, it's just weird to think....

EVELYN: People do it all the time. Especially out *here...*

ADAM: Right, no, you're right, I just never imagined myself one of those people....

EVELYN: I'm one of those people. Would you ever've guessed that?

ADAM: What? You are not....

EVELYN: Bullshit. Take a look...

ADAM: Where...? *(He moves over to her, studies her nose.)* I don't see anything.

EVELYN: Exactly.

ADAM: You had your nose done? Honestly?

EVELYN: At sixteen. My parents' birthday present...

ADAM: Thoughtful.

EVELYN: No, I asked for it. I had this terrible hook. "The Jewish Slope," we called it in Lake Forest... the only ski run for miles around!

ADAM: *(Smiling)* I can't believe it...I can't tell....

EVELYN: That's the idea, isn't it?

ADAM: Yeah, but...you could be lying to me.

EVELYN: And what would be the point of that?

ADAM: To get me in here. To watch chunks of my flesh get torn away...you could be a sadist, for all I know....

EVELYN: Hey, quit sweet-talking to me....

ADAM: Well, they did an amazing job. *(Beat)* Wait a minute, your name's "Thompson," that's not Jewish....

EVELYN: On my mother's side, you dope. That's what makes me Jewish...her maiden name is "Tessman."

ADAM: Oh.

EVELYN: We don't have to stay here, Adam....

ADAM: No, it's alright, it just makes me a little jumpy....

EVELYN: It's cosmetic, not corrective...it's no big deal. I promise....

ADAM: If it's cosmetic, why can't I just put some powder on it or something, or shade it in on the side like they do for Richard Gere in photos....

EVELYN: You mean, before?

ADAM: ...he had it done?!

EVELYN: Take a look at *American Gigolo* and then at any picture of him today. I'm serious. Lots of guys do it...Joel Grey.

ADAM: Okay, that's it, let's go....

EVELYN: *(Laughing)* Kidding! What about Sting?

ADAM: Yeah, I knew he did. Looked totally different in *Quadrophenia*. I used to rent that video all the time, my "Mod" phase....

EVELYN: That must've been cute.... *(Beat)* Does he look better now? Sting, I mean?

ADAM: I suppose so...maybe it's just all that yoga, though.

EVELYN: I think you'll look great. You have a good face, a nice shape to your nose, actually, but it's just got that bit of....

ADAM: What?

EVELYN: ...bulb...at the end. Not a bulb, exactly, but...

ADAM: No, I got it, sort of the "Rudolph" effect. At least I can guide your sleigh tonight....

EVELYN: You can guide my sleigh any night.

(They look at one another, kiss.)

ADAM: P D A.

EVELYN: Indeed...

ADAM: Shall I check the men's room?

EVELYN: I dare you....

ADAM: Shut up!

EVELYN: I'm serious....

ADAM: You're crazy....

EVELYN: Quite possibly. I still dare you....

ADAM: What if they call us?

EVELYN: Then they'll just have to wait, won't they?

ADAM: I suppose they would....

EVELYN: Can you afford to be late, that's the question. Will you take the risk...?

ADAM: Is this, like, my last meal or something? A conjugal visit before I'm drawn and quartered....

EVELYN: Stop being so morbid...it's just flesh.

ADAM: Yeah, I see what you mean..."It's just flesh," that's not morbid at all.

EVELYN: It isn't. It's one of the most perfect substances on earth. Natural, beautiful. Think about it...

ADAM: I'd rather not.

EVELYN: Oh come on...you've bitten more skin off from around your fingernails than a doctor would ever trim off your nose. It's true....

ADAM: Yeah, but that's just....

EVELYN: ...what? It's the same thing. Now, that grows back and this wouldn't, but that's about the only difference. *(Beat)* How did you get that scar on your back?

ADAM: Which, the...?

EVELYN: Yes. The raised one....

ADAM: A kid, ummm, threw a stick at me...first grade.

EVELYN: Stitches?

ADAM: Yeah. Thirty-three...

EVELYN: And is that terrible? Are you disfigured because of it...?

ADAM: Well, I don't like to wear tanktops....

EVELYN: ...and you should be respected for that....

ADAM: *(Giggling)* I'm serious...it bugs me....

EVELYN: Okay, but why? Because it looks ugly or because you think other people will think it looks bad? Which?

ADAM: I dunno....

EVELYN: What's the matter with scars? Not a thing... *(Pulls up sleeve)* Look at these, see there?

ADAM: What're those?

EVELYN: They're scars...lots of little scars. You didn't notice them before?

ADAM: Yeah, I guess I did, but I didn't think anything....

EVELYN: Sure, you did. Of course you would, they're on my wrist. You know what they are....

ADAM: ...did you try to...?

EVELYN: No, not really. I mean, I cut on myself a little, tried to get attention when I was a teenager, but I didn't want to slit my veins open. Or I would have....

ADAM: Oh.

EVELYN: I'm a very straightforward person.

ADAM: Yeah, I'm getting that....

EVELYN: It's the only way to be. Why lie?

ADAM: You're right.

EVELYN: Exactly. *(Beat)* So, is my arm unattractive to you, then, because of those, or not? Tell me...

ADAM: No...

EVELYN: Are you lying?

ADAM: No, not at all, I love your arm.

EVELYN: "Love" is a big word....

ADAM: I know that. That's why I used it. I don't throw it around, believe me....

EVELYN: Either do I.

ADAM: I love your arm. It's beautiful....
(He takes hold of her wrist gently, kisses it.)

EVELYN: They're like rings on a tree. They signify experience...make us unique.

ADAM: I can see that.

EVELYN: And that's all this is, the idea of you having some surgery. It's an experience....

ADAM: I know, it just makes me....

EVELYN: ...what, nervous? Of course you should be nervous, why not? It's something you've never done...but that's the adventure.

ADAM: "It's a far, far better thing I do than I have ever done..."

EVELYN: Something like that. Is that from a book?

ADAM: Yeah, Dickens...

EVELYN: Huh. Well, I don't know about better, but at least different.

(Another quick kiss.)

EVELYN: So, are you gonna go check?

ADAM: What? ...You mean, the rest room?

EVELYN: Uh-huh.

ADAM: Ummm...okay. What if they call my name, though? Seriously...

EVELYN: What if they do?

ADAM: *(Smiling)* I smell trouble...which I may not be able to do after this.

EVELYN: Just go...

ADAM: *(Standing)* Okay, why not? Then I can show you something....

EVELYN: What?

ADAM: Just a little thing I had done. For you.

EVELYN: Wait, what...show me now.

(He looks around, can't wait. He pulls open his pants and lets her glance inside.)

ADAM: Look...a big religious no-no. *(Pulls at his waistband)* Nice, huh?

EVELYN: "Eat." Lemme guess...you couldn't afford the "me."

ADAM: No, you goof! Your *initials*. Like it?

EVELYN: *(Touching it)* I do, I like it. And I love the gesture....

ADAM: "Love" is a big word.

EVELYN: I know that. That's why I used it.... *(Beat)* Go check the "handicapped" stall. I'm suddenly very hungry....

(He slips off, out of the waiting room. EVELYN goes back to reading her magazine, when a voice calls out.)

VOICE: Mr Sorenson. Adam Sorenson, please...

(EVELYN looks up, glances toward where ADAM has disappeared but says nothing. She smiles.)

(The lawn)

(A stretch of green hidden near a graveled path. Trees sway overhead. Benches in clusters at gracious intervals.)

(PHILLIP and ADAM sitting on their jackets between classes, talking. PHILLIP has a a pair of sunglasses perched on his head. ADAM has a bandage across his nose.)

PHILLIP: ...I'm serious, it looks good.

ADAM: Just shut up...don't get here late and then make fun of me.

PHILLIP: No, you look distinguished.

ADAM: Phil, I look like a hockey player....

PHILLIP: Yeah, but a distinguished one.

(They chuckle.)

PHILLIP: What'd you do, anyway?

ADAM: ...I fell.

PHILLIP: Come on...

ADAM: Seriously, I did....

PHILLIP: You sound like a battered wife. "I fell...."

ADAM: That's not funny.

PHILLIP: Yeah, it is...it's very funny. I mean, it's not that funny that wives get beat up, but the fact that you look like one, that I find hilarious....

ADAM: Well, anyway, that's what happened. I tripped, I fell...no big deal.

PHILLIP: Sure it wasn't the bathroom door?
That's the usual excuse....

ADAM: For who?

PHILLIP: Abused women...

ADAM: You're sick.

PHILLIP: Somewhat, yeah. But I'm nice-looking,
which makes up for a lot.

ADAM: Not as much as you think....

PHILLIP: 'Don't hate me because I'm beautiful."

ADAM: I don't...I just hate you.

PHILLIP: See, I knew you did, all these years.... *(Beat)*
You really fell?

ADAM: Yeah. I tripped on the stairs going into my
apartment and caught my face on the...you know...the....

PHILLIP: No, what?

ADAM: Oh, come on! It's not that fascinating....

PHILLIP: It is, too. It's completely fascinating.
So, you don't wanna tell me then, right?

ADAM: Tell you what?!

PHILLIP: What happened to your...

ADAM: I told you. I tripped going up the...and hit the
edge of the....

PHILLIP: Yeah, it's the "edge of" that I'm a little hazy on
here....

ADAM: Edge of the knob. My door knob.

PHILLIP: She clocked you one, didn't she?

ADAM: Who?

PHILLIP: "Who?" The artist, formerly known as Evelyn,
or whatever her name is....

ADAM: Are you nuts?

PHILLIP: Well, I've gotta hand it to her, she certainly made a "statement"....

ADAM: You are such an idiot....

PHILLIP: Did she hit you?

ADAM: Stop!

PHILLIP: I don't care if she did, I'm just asking....

ADAM: Yeah, well...you can be annoying.

PHILLIP: It's one of my best qualities, actually....

ADAM: And there aren't many of them.

PHILLIP: You really tripped? Truthfully...

ADAM: Yes.

PHILLIP: ...huh. Okay.

ADAM: Why do you say that? "Huh." You don't believe me?

PHILLIP: No, I just...nothing.

ADAM: What? Don't do that, come on now. What?

PHILLIP: It's no big.... *(Beat)* I saw your girlfriend the other day, maybe, what, last Thursday? You weren't in class, and I said to her, I asked her if you were okay, that's all....

ADAM: Yeah, so?

PHILLIP: And she said "yes," but you were recovering from an operation or something....

ADAM: What?!

PHILLIP: That what I said, "he didn't tell me about anything," and she said it wasn't really an operation *per se*, just some thing you had done. A procedure. And that was it...so I just thought....

ADAM: No, it's not....

PHILLIP: Hey, you don't have to tell me, we're not on intimate terms or anything....

ADAM: I hurt it. Really...

PHILLIP: Whatever.

ADAM: No, not "whatever." Phil...I did. I hit it and, you know...I banged it pretty bad at home and so I had the doctor look at it. But he didn't...*operate* or anything. The bandage is from that. The door.

PHILLIP: After you tripped on the stairs...yeah, you told me.

ADAM: She must've just gotten confused.

PHILLIP: Maybe. That doesn't seem to happen to her very often, though...she's pretty sharp.

ADAM: No, she is...I'm sure it's just the way I explained it. I mean, to her....

PHILLIP: Right.

ADAM: ...and where did you see her?

PHILLIP: Evelyn? I don't know...Starbucks or somewhere. The mall, maybe.

ADAM: She doesn't drink coffee.

PHILLIP: So, it was downtown then, Record City, I think.... *(Beat)* What, you worried I'm gonna steal her? Believe me...

ADAM: No, God...don't be so... *(Touches nose)* Anyway, it's gonna be fine....

PHILLIP: Well, that's good to hear.

ADAM: Yep.

PHILLIP: ...so you're okay, though?

ADAM: No. I mean, yeah, I'm great...absolutely.

PHILLIP: Then good... *(Beat)* And you'd tell me if there was anything seriously wrong?

ADAM: ...of course! Hey, what's up?

PHILLIP: I mean, we're friends, right? You'd come to me....

ADAM: ...about what? *(Beat)* Phil, what's...?

PHILLIP: Jenny told me.

ADAM: What?

(ADAM *looks at his friend. For the first time,* PHILLIP *seems less than in control.)*

PHILLIP: She kissed you.

ADAM: Oh.

PHILLIP: She felt shitty, I guess. I could tell for, like, a week that something was going on and finally she told me about it. How you guys met and talked about us—why do girls always have to *talk* about everything?—and later she leaned over and kissed you. That's what she told me.

ADAM: She did...I mean, she did do that but it was nothing.

PHILLIP: Hey, it wasn't nothing, she's a good kisser. Hell of a kisser.

ADAM: I don't mean "nothing," but it meant nothing. It didn't hold any meaning for us...it just happened.

PHILLIP: Okay. So, you can speak for her, then?

ADAM: For me...it didn't for me. It was just a... that's all she said?

PHILLIP: Don't tell me there's more....

ADAM: No, God, not at all...I just....

PHILLIP: It's alright, I'd been acting weird lately, this whole marriage idea is just...freaky...so, it's my fault.

ADAM: Right...

PHILLIP: I mean, who gets married at *twenty-two* these days? Right? It's not the Middle Ages, for Chrissakes.... *(Beat)* I just feel bad...you know, for her.

ADAM: Why?

PHILLIP: Kissing you...that's hideous! It's what those new-age dumbshits would call "a desperate cry for help"....

(They laugh, catching each other's eye.)

ADAM: Sorry...

PHILLIP: 'S alright. It's better than me having to kiss you....

ADAM: Good point.

PHILLIP: No tongue, right?

ADAM: Jesus...

PHILLIP: I'm just asking....

ADAM: No! Please...

(PHILLIP looks at his watch.)

PHILLIP: Well, I got a three-ten. "International Cinema" or some shit.

ADAM: Yeah?

PHILLIP: I guess...it's an elective, I just show up for the tests. You?

ADAM: Nah...I'm free. Gonna go work out.

PHILLIP: You and the...what is going on with the "metamorphosis" thing here? You're like Frankenstein....

ADAM: You mean, Frankenstein's monster.
Frankenstein was the doctor....

PHILLIP: Ahh, don't be such an English Lit prick...

ADAM: I am an English Lit prick.

PHILLIP: I know, but you don't have to sound like one,
do you? Doctor, monster, whatever! What's up with
that?

ADAM: Nothing. It feels good.

PHILLIP: How much weight have you lost?

ADAM: Not that much, maybe ten pounds or...

PHILLIP: I'd say more like fifteen.

ADAM: Yeah, maybe.

PHILLIP: And the hair thing going, no glasses now....

ADAM: It's just a few little....

PHILLIP: Hey, it's the "new you." Plus, the nails.
Jenny told me that, which is the one thing that I
just cannot believe!

ADAM: It's a life change....

PHILLIP: Please, don't make me throw up with the
Oprah-talk, alright? I'm trying to compliment you
here....

ADAM: ...thanks.

PHILLIP: I used to find blood on our *phone*, okay,
so it's not just this casual thing, quitting....

ADAM: I know. I know that....

PHILLIP: Alright, then. *(Beat)* No, you look good. I can
see why she kissed you...hell, I might even kiss you,
with a few drinks in me.

ADAM: *(Laughing)* I'll run home and hide the liquor....

PHILLIP: Please, I'll help you! *(Beat)* And nothing else happened, right, I mean, between you and Jenny?

(ADAM *stops cold. Walked right into a trap.)*

ADAM: ...what?

PHILLIP: I'm just asking.

ADAM: Phil...

PHILLIP: Not really looking for a speech or anything. Just an answer. She said "no," just so you don't think I'm laying a trap here or whatever....

ADAM: I don't.

PHILLIP: ...nobody saw you on campus or anything. A lifeguard out by the dunes, you know, so....

ADAM: ...what's that supposed to mean?

PHILLIP: I'm just *saying*, I'll believe you, whatever you tell me. I've got no witnesses. So...

ADAM: Nothing happened, Phil. Truthfully.

PHILLIP: ...that's not what she said.

(ADAM *freezes but doesn't falter.)*

ADAM: That's not true.

PHILLIP: You sure?

ADAM: Yes.

PHILLIP: You're right, it's not true. Hey, a man's gotta try....

ADAM: Uh-huh...

PHILLIP: Not that I want out of this or anything. I love scuba-diving....

ADAM: Of course. As we all do....

PHILLIP: Exactly. I'm just not sure I wanna share my air tank with the same person the rest of my life....

(ADAM *says nothing, just smiles.*)

PHILLIP: ...but that's my problem. *(Beat)* I gotta get to class....

ADAM: Alright. Take care.

PHILLIP: Sorry for the, you know, crazy shit.

ADAM: It's okay....

PHILLIP: ...don't kiss my girlfriend any more, alright?

ADAM: You got it.

PHILLIP: See you...we should do something again one of these days, all of us, I mean....

ADAM: ...yeah...

PHILLIP: If you guys wanna. Let us know. So long, Romeo!

ADAM: *(Pulling on a coat)* Knock it off!

(PHILLIP *starts off but stops dead. He turns back and studies* ADAM.)

PHILLIP: ...where's your jacket?

ADAM: What?

PHILLIP: Okay, this is too much. The cord jacket, the lumberjacky-looking thing...

ADAM: I dunno...anyway, it's not a jacket, it's a blazer.

PHILLIP: Uh-huh. And this, umm, Tommy Hilfiger-ish job, where'd you come up with that?

ADAM: ...the mall. I bought it.

PHILLIP: *You* bought some clothes? You, like, went out to the mall on your bike and actually....

ADAM: No, Evelyn drove me. So? What's the big...?

PHILLIP: The deal is this...you've had that frumpy-looking fucker for three years, probably more,

and I've never seen you out of it. *Ever.* Middle of
California, the dead of *summer*, whatever, you've got
that coat on. And now you're just like, "Hey, whatever,
(Yawns) yeah, I bought the ol' stars and stripes here
with Evelyn." That's like a sailing slicker!

ADAM: It's their yachtsman line....

PHILLIP: I am gonna puke here, I swear to God! I did
not just hear you use the word "yachtsman"....

ADAM: Hey, she likes it.... *(Opens jacket)* It's reversible

PHILLIP: Well, isn't that just neat? And peachy keen
and whatever other *Little House On The Prairie* shit you
wanna spout...what I wanna know is, do you like it?

ADAM: ...it's okay.

PHILLIP: Not what I said. I asked, "do-you-like-it?"

ADAM: It's fine. It's a coat....

PHILLIP: And lemme ask you...did you get to keep the
cord job or did she make you toss it?

ADAM: ...who cares? This is...I threw it out, okay?
Goodwill, actually.

PHILLIP: "Goodwill, actually."

ADAM: It's really no big thing....

PHILLIP: Dude, don't just say "no big thing." I begged
you to throw out the "blazer" our Freshman year,
I mean, you've lost *both* of us a lot of dates with that
thing on! You've had it since, like, birth, okay, so do
me a little favor and let's not pretend that the jacket and
the, ahh, weight and the Jon Bon Jovi hair are no big
deal. Because when it comes to routine, you used to be
like Mister goddamn *Rogers!*

ADAM: Phil, it's a fucking jacket so just lay off. Go to
class...

PHILLIP: Uh-huh. Fine...

ADAM: Fine.

PHILLIP: I just hope next time we pass each other I recognize who the hell you are....

ADAM: Well, if not, you and Evelyn can always head over to Record City and have a chat....

PHILLIP: Hey, I wouldn't get too deep into the moral issues during this particular conversation...okay, Romeo? I may have a big fucking mouth, but at least I keep it to myself....

(They stare at each other, a nearly visible wall going up between them. ADAM blinks first and walks off. PHILLIP watches him go.)

PHILLIP: So long, matey!

(The coffee shop)

(A local Starbucks knockoff, with lots of cozy nooks and corners in its bi-level design. Glass lamps hang overhead.)

(EVELYN stands with JENNY at a high table, sipping hot drinks.)

EVELYN: ...and you, everything's good?

JENNY: Yeah, you know. Okay.

EVELYN: Huh. Well, that's nice to hear....

JENNY: You?

EVELYN: Oh, you know, pretty great. Just studying, working on my art...

JENNY: Right, you've got a big thing you're doing, or, what do you call it?

EVELYN: Thesis project. For my degree...

JENNY: That's terrific.

EVELYN: Yeah. The showing's in a couple weeks....

JENNY: And it's going well? What is it again?

EVELYN: I never said....

JENNY: Oh, well, that's why.

EVELYN: Right. *(Beat)* It's this sculpture thingie....

JENNY: "Thingie." That's one of Adam's words...

EVELYN: You oughta know.

JENNY: ...mmmm, I love the arts.

EVELYN: Really?

JENNY: Yeah, you know, going to movies and stuff.
We don't get so many here, we have to drive into the
city for any of the new releases, but I see a lot of videos.
Phil watches 'em constantly.

EVELYN: Yeah, and what kind does he like?

JENNY: Oh, a bunch, but more artsy ones than I do...
Aliens. Stargate. The Twelve Monkeys. Is that right,
or were there ten of 'em?

EVELYN: No, it was twelve...a dozen monkeys,
all together.

JENNY: Anyway, that kind. Sci-fi, but with some
meaning, too. And action.

EVELYN: Huh. That's great...I hate sci-fi. *(Beat)*
And you? What kind do you like, Jenny?

JENNY: Ummm, any, I don't mind...but I usually like at
least some romance in them. That's always nice.

(EVELYN *studies her for a moment.*)

EVELYN: Yes...romance's good. Especially when you
least expect it.

JENNY: Uh-huh...

(JENNY *looks over, sees that* EVELYN *is watching her,
looks away quickly.*)

JENNY: ...you know, I was gonna say, I think what
you've done with Adam, it's really great.

EVELYN: And what've I done?

JENNY: You know, just...he's changed.

EVELYN: That's right. *He's* changed.

JENNY: That's what I mean.

EVELYN: He's done the work....

JENNY: Of course, I didn't mean that you....

EVELYN: I know. I'm just saying, he did it.

JENNY: Right. That's always what they say, though, isn't it?

EVELYN: What? And who are they?

JENNY: You know, like, in *Cosmo*, when they have those tests, asking what you'd like to change about your guy....

EVELYN: Ahhh. Now you're gonna get all scientific on me....

JENNY: It's true, though, right? Almost everybody I've gone out with, if you could alter just one thing, or even get them to stop wearing sunglasses up on their head all the time...then they'd be perfect. It's that sort of deal, isn't it?

EVELYN: Something like that...or it could just be that I care about him.

JENNY: Phil's got, like, six of those "one things," but it's the same idea....

EVELYN: Right. And how is ol' Phil?

JENNY: He's...Phil. Six "things" away from being amazing...

(ADAM *arrives at the table, obviously unprepared to find both women waiting for him. He wears no bandage.*)

ADAM: ...hey, Evelyn. Hi. Jenny, hello.

EVELYN/JENNY: Hi, Adam. Hello.

ADAM: I didn't know you guys were....

EVELYN: I invited her.

ADAM: That's alright, then....

JENNY: I like your new jacket! Phil told me about it....

ADAM: Oh, right. Yeah. It's...new.

JENNY: And your nose! God, you okay?

ADAM: Yep. 'Course...it was nothing.

JENNY: Falling down's not nothing. *(Studies him)* Looks okay, though...

(An uncomfortable pause. EVELYN *looks over at* ADAM, *who clears his throat.)*

EVELYN: You *fell*?

ADAM: ...yeah. Anyway...

EVELYN: Anyway, pull up some floor...we got you a cocoa.

(He moves warily to them, squeezing in next to EVELYN.*)*

ADAM: Thanks. *(To* EVELYN*)* You don't drink coffee....

EVELYN: It's not. It's decaf....

ADAM: That's still coffee.

EVELYN: Good point. So I drink coffee, then, I just don't like the caffeine....

JENNY: Me either.

EVELYN: Really? You don't like caffeine, either, Jenny? Did you know that, too, Adam, that Jenny doesn't like caffeine?

ADAM: No. I didn't know that....

EVELYN: See? There's lots you don't know....

(They all sip their drinks silently for a moment.)

EVELYN: Jenny was just saying that she thinks you're great...I mean, doing great things with yourself.

ADAM: Yeah? Thanks, Jenny...

JENNY: You're welcome. I just....

EVELYN: She thinks you're just about perfect now, don't you, Jen?

JENNY: I didn't say that.

EVELYN: So, he's not perfect, then? Obviously his motor control's a bit off, if he fell, but....

JENNY: I said that you guys are....

ADAM: Forget about it.

EVELYN: It's true, I'm exaggerating. She said, and I paraphrase, "He's changed." But she implied for the better....

ADAM: Well, I agree. I have. And again, thank you.

JENNY: Welcome...

EVELYN: I think you've changed, too, Adam. A lot.

ADAM: Yeah? How's that?

EVELYN: Well, I mean, it's obvious, all the minor things are pretty obvious, but in subtler ways as well... you've gotten cuter. And stronger. More confident. And craftier...

ADAM: "Craftier," huh?

EVELYN: Apparently so...that spill you took must've done it.

JENNY: I'm sorry, am I missing something?

ADAM: I'm not sure.... (*To* EVELYN) Evelyn, what's up?

EVELYN: Nothing. Not a thing...

JENNY: I mean, you knew about him hurting himself, didn't you? (*To* ADAM) Phil said you had a big bandage on, so I just figured....

EVELYN: No, Jenny, I saw it. I'm kidding....

JENNY: Ahh. I couldn't tell....

EVELYN: Sometimes it's hard to read me. Know when I'm joking....

ADAM: Very hard.

EVELYN: It is. But I am...joking, I mean. Adam took a bad fall and smashed his nose, but he's okay now...see?

(She grabs ADAM's *face and holds it out for* JENNY *to look.* ADAM *pulls away, a bit too quickly.)*

EVELYN: ...it healed well, don't you think?

JENNY: Yes.

ADAM: Do you guys wanna salad or something? I'm hungry....

EVELYN: I'm fine. Jenny...hungry?

JENNY: I'm okay. *(To* ADAM*)* Your nose looks... how much weight have you lost?

ADAM: Not that much, really.

EVELYN: Twenty-one pounds. *(To* ADAM*)* I peeked, is that alright?

(He glares at her; JENNY *tries to keep up.)*

JENNY: Peeked?

EVELYN: His journal...a record of his progress that he's keeping. Twenty-one pounds as of...

ADAM: ...last Friday. Yeah.

JENNY: Really? That's so cool....

EVELYN: *Cosmo* story in the making, huh?

JENNY: Yep.

ADAM: It's good, yeah, I've been keeping at it....

EVELYN: She knows, Adam, she already said you've "changed." And I already agreed. We're past that....

ADAM: Okay, I'm, like, totally lost here....

EVELYN: You're mentioned in there, too, Jenny.

JENNY: Where?

EVELYN: Adam's journal. I mean, it's a veiled entry but I think it's you....

ADAM: Evelyn...

EVELYN: I peeked twice. *(To* JENNY*)* You're right next to someone known as "cute waitress."

JENNY: *(Cautiously)* ...why's that? I mean...Adam?

ADAM: You're not. It's...she's....

EVELYN: Something about a meeting...and a drive after, in your cute little V-dub....

ADAM: What're you saying?! Jenny, there's not any....

*(*JENNY *picks up her purse and smiles thinly.)*

JENNY: You know what? It's pretty late, I should get....

ADAM: No, don't go.... *(To* EVELYN*)* Why are you doing this?

EVELYN: I'm just having coffee. Decaf.

JENNY: I need to go.

EVELYN: I just wanna talk about the kiss. Why can't we do that?

(The moment hangs. JENNY *stops short.)*

EVELYN: We should just put it out there...I'm very open, and I just feel that....

ADAM: This is inappropriate, okay?

JENNY: *(To* ADAM*)* Did you tell her about the...?

EVELYN: No, no, he didn't...Phillip did. We met and he told me all about it, Jenny. What you told him, anyway. The rest I got from lover boy's diary....

JENNY: ...Adam?

ADAM: She's making that up...she's....

EVELYN: Am I?

ADAM: Yes!

EVELYN: Then set the record straight...

ADAM: I don't wanna do this right now.

EVELYN: Seems a touch late for that.

JENNY: *(To* EVELYN*)* Phillip told you about our talk? When? *(Beat)* What else did he tell you?

EVELYN: Lots of things...he's a very chatty guy, when you wind him up.

JENNY: ...I can't believe it....

EVELYN: Then you're never gonna believe the rest of this....

ADAM: Evelyn, let's just drop it, okay? If you're angry with me, alright, but this is not....

EVELYN: We're just talking. People need to share more, that's how this stuff happens, this covert stuff, because we hide it....

JENNY: Fine...you want to...go ahead. Adam wrote something in his journal, obviously, and I told Phil about....

ADAM: Jenny, I didn't....

JENNY: What do you wanna hear? We kissed.

EVELYN: No, I knew that...I'm sorry, I've confused you. I meant about my kiss. With Phillip. That's the part I wanted to talk about with you guys...I didn't make that clear?

JENNY: ...what?

ADAM: That's bullshit....

EVELYN: No, that's getting even. *(Beat)* Unless you guys have something else to tell me. Meaning, "the drive"...

ADAM: We didn't go on any....

JENNY: That's not true. You didn't meet Phil....

EVELYN: Ask him.

JENNY: ...or he would've told me...he....

EVELYN: Apparently not.

JENNY: ...I'm going. I'm going now, 'kay? *(Beat)* I'll...see you. Adam, I'm....

EVELYN: *(Calling to her)* You guys are still coming to my showing, right? Phillip said you would!

(She is gone. ADAM *takes a careful sip before speaking. He turns to* EVELYN, *about to speak, when* JENNY *returns.)*

JENNY: *(Directly at* EVELYN*)* Hey...look, I don't know why I'm here, I guess I came back to say "I'm sorry." Sorry if I've offended you in some way, or done something to make you so indifferent to me, cold or whatever. And I don't mean what's happened, I don't, because I think you've been this way the whole time I've known you. So...sorry I'm not an artsy person or cool enough, sorry about that. But as far as just *being* a person, like, an average-type person...I'm pretty okay. I am. *(Beat)* That kinda came out bad, I mean, dumb, so I'm just gonna...yeah. *(She wanders off.)*

ADAM: ...okay, that was horrible.

EVELYN: Oh, I dunno...I could've told her about the blow job I gave him. *(Beat)* Kidding...

ADAM: No, listen, what you did was shitty, and awful and just plain wrong....

EVELYN: As opposed to you two sneaking off and making out? Where would that fall on the "bad behaviour" list...?

ADAM: You had no right to do that.

EVELYN: True.

ADAM: Make her feel that way...

EVELYN: She's got a boyfriend who's shit. Now she knows. Hell, she already knew....

ADAM: It was still wrong to treat her like that! And me.

EVELYN: Yeah, let's talk about you....

ADAM: Go ahead. You seem raring to go.

EVELYN: You wanna tell me about the rest of your date, or should I...?

ADAM: She called me, okay, asked if I could get together and talk, you know, about Phil. And them.

EVELYN: And then you made out. Most natural thing in the world...

ADAM: Look, I was going to say something...it just happened.

EVELYN: That was Hitler's excuse. Try another one...

ADAM: It was a mistake! Okay? I know that....

EVELYN: And how *big* was that mistake? (*Beat*) I don't care about what happened. I don't. I just want the truth...I told you about what I did—you think I wanted to kiss that guy?—I only did it for the effect. But I'm asking you...what else went on? I deserve to know.

ADAM: ...nothing.

EVELYN: You're sticking with that?

ADAM: Yes.

EVELYN: Even if I tell you I know something else went on.

ADAM: How could you? It didn't...and I did not put any "drive" in my journal. That was a lie.

EVELYN: No, it was a *bluff*. Because I could sense it.... *(Beat)* And the waitress *was* there....

ADAM: I'm telling the truth. About Jenny, I mean....

EVELYN: I don't believe you.

ADAM: ...I am!

EVELYN: Then we'll have to leave it at that. Won't we?

(They stare at one another. She touches her nose.)

EVELYN: Oh, and glad to hear about your trip...see you next fall.

ADAM: That's a bad joke....

EVELYN: It's a worse lie....

ADAM: What was I gonna tell them? Huh?

EVELYN: The truth?

ADAM: Come on...I took shit about my new jacket! That's all people say to me any more, "What's up with you? What's going on?" I can't exactly spread it around about what I've done....

EVELYN: What? You *fell*....

ADAM: What're we doing here?

EVELYN: I dunno. You tell me....

ADAM: I don't know. I really don't....

EVELYN: Are you tired of me? 'S that it?

ADAM: God, no! Are you nuts?!

EVELYN: Then I don't get it...I don't wanna sound old-fashioned here, but you're a step away from fucking around on me....

ADAM: I would never do that....

EVELYN: No, you would never do that with *her*, and mostly because she wouldn't. I know the type, she

needed a shoulder, well, what the hell, why not a kiss
while she's at it, and maybe a quick hand job. Who
knows? But she's not gonna screw you and you
probably wouldn't be able to get it up, anyway,
because he's your best "bud." *(Beat)* But lemme ask
you, Adam, if it hadn't been her, if it'd been, oh,
say that "cute waitress" the other night....

(ADAM looks away; EVELYN doesn't let up.)

EVELYN: ...didn't think I caught that, did you? The
chatty-chat and the extra three bucks on the tip.

ADAM: ...that was nothing.

EVELYN: It's never anything. Until it's something....
(Beat) If it'd been her instead...out on that drive....

ADAM: ...we-didn't-go-for-a....

EVELYN: ...whatever. But if she'd been there instead,
then what? Just ask yourself.

ADAM: Jesus, next you're gonna tell me the
handkerchief with the strawberries on it is missing....

EVELYN: I don't know that reference.

ADAM: Don't worry about it. *(Pleads)* Evelyn, please...

(She smiles and begins more gently.)

EVELYN: I just wanna know where we stand...
I thought I could trust you.

ADAM: You can!

EVELYN: She's your friend's fiancée, Adam.
I'm your girlfriend...where's the trust in that?

(He takes her hand suddenly.)

ADAM: I'll do anything you want. Okay? I know what
I did was wrong, I do, I messed up but I've never done
that before. Lied to a person I was going out with...shit,
I haven't even gone out with someone for the two years

before we met! So, tell me what to do and I'll do it...
I just, I just don't wanna lose you.

EVELYN: You're sure...?

ADAM: I am so sure. I love you....

EVELYN: I told you, that's a big word....

ADAM: ...and I'm using it. I do, completely.

EVELYN: Anything I say?

ADAM: Anything.

EVELYN: *(Without emotion)* Give them up. As friends,
both of them. No explanation. Don't see them or speak
to them again. Not ever.

ADAM: ...huh?

EVELYN: That's what I want. That's the proof to me
about how you feel....

ADAM: Evelyn...that's....

EVELYN: One should always be careful when asking to
be put to a test....

ADAM: ...Jesus Christ...

EVELYN: So, what's it gonna be, Adam?

ADAM: And if I don't...?

EVELYN: Pretty much like these things end. I mean,
in life, at least...if this was a movie, I'd see the light
eventually, but no such luck. Final answer?

(ADAM stares at her for a long moment.)

ADAM: ...I choose you.

(She pulls him close and kisses him for a long time.)

EVELYN: You choose well, grasshopper....

(The auditorium)

(Gorgeous Art-Deco affair, with rich carpets and sconces on the wall. Framed posters of theater productions and concerts.)

*(*PHILLIP *standing around, dressed up and Ray-Bans on his head.* ADAM *enters, smartly dressed and wearing his new jacket reversed. He sees* PHILLIP *and tries to go the other way.)*

PHILLIP: ...Adam, hey. *(Spots jacket)* Ahoy...

ADAM: *(Looking around)* Hey, Phil. How's it going?

PHILLIP: You know, okay. So, what, you don't take my calls now?

ADAM: No, I've been...I mean....

PHILLIP: 'S okay, I understand. The whole...thing...

ADAM: Nah, it's just been busy lately. At work and stuff...

PHILLIP: Yeah. Whatever.

ADAM: Seriously. *(Beat)* I need to get a seat....

PHILLIP: Hold on, hey...where's the fire?

ADAM: *(Nervously)* I just wanna...good spot. *(Beat)* Where's Jenny?

PHILLIP: Funny.

ADAM: What?

PHILLIP: Man, come on...we broke up. Broke it off, whatever. You knew that.

ADAM: What? No, I, when...?

PHILLIP: Like, two weeks ago...right after...you know. And I'm sorry about that. I was pissed off, but, I mean...no call for that "eye for an eye" shit.

ADAM: ...it's okay. But you and Jenny're...? I can't believe that.

PHILLIP: Believe it. *(Beat)* She came over one day, after seeing you guys, I guess, and that was it. The ring off, took her C Ds back and gone.

ADAM: ...I'm sorry.

PHILLIP: Listen, no hard feelings...I was looking to get out, you know that. But once you start making those plans, you know, like picking out *napkins* and shit, it's almost easier to just do the thing! *(Beat)* You did me a favour, really...too young to get hitched.

ADAM: I don't know what to say....

PHILLIP: Don't worry about it. *(Beat)* You haven't seen her lately, have you? Jenny, I mean....

ADAM: No...

PHILLIP: 'Kay. Anyway, this oughta be good, huh?!

(They share a light laugh. JENNY *walks up the aisle, sees them and goes for a seat.)*

ADAM: Jenny, hi...

JENNY: Oh, Adam...hello. Hi, Phil.

PHILLIP: Hey.

ADAM: I'm sorry about...you guys....

JENNY: *(Glaring at* PHILLIP*)* Boy, you just can't keep anything to yourself, can you?

PHILLIP: What?

JENNY: You never change...that's what. *(She starts to walk off but stops, turning back around.)* Oh, and Phil?

PHILLIP: Yeah?

JENNY: You don't really *need* sunglasses at night....

(She smiles and moves off, taking a place down front. ADAM and PHILLIP watch her go; PHILLIP cursing quietly to himself.)

ADAM: What's she...?

PHILLIP: It's not, like, totally *official* yet...ahh, fuck, what're you gonna do?

(The lights flicker twice. ADAM looks up.)

ADAM: We should find a place to....

PHILLIP: *(Looking)* There's two over there.

ADAM: Umm...maybe we shouldn't....

PHILLIP: ...got it. Whatever. Take care, man.

(He wanders off. ADAM watches him go, then moves down to find a place to sit.)

(The house lights flicker, theatrical lights up. After a moment, EVELYN [Dressed up for her] enters crisply on stage and smiles. Two large easels tower on either side of her.)

EVELYN: Good evening. Thank you for coming out tonight—it's the middle of finals and I'm sure this is not how most of you would choose to spend your time away from campus...*on* campus. So, I promise to make this presentation as quick and painless as possible and get you back home as swiftly as I can. The accompanying visual portion of this graduate thesis project is currently under review but will hopefully be available in the exhibition gallery down the hall for your perusal next week, so if you don't stay tonight for punch and cookies, ummm, please stop by and take a look at your convenience. *(Smiles)* Okay, that's the

boring stuff.... *(She turns over a note card.)* My task here
tonight is to unveil my semester's work, explain it and
then smile and shake hands, leaving a few of you to
examine it, grade it, etc. In essence, be at your mercy.
Here at "Mercy." *(Laughs)* Which is fine, since I realize
I have been my entire academic life—at someone's
mercy, that is—which reaches back to when I was five.
So be it...that's the system and one person can't change
it...but perhaps they can make you question that system
and your values just a little bit. *(Looks over cards)*
Blah-blah-blah... *(She starts to move but steps back into
the light, as if she's forgotten something.)* Oh, I almost
forgot...and this is fairly personal, probably shouldn't
even do it but it really is the capper to my time here at
Mercy, so please indulge me. *(Beat)* I was given an
engagement ring two days ago and I haven't answered
the guy yet...So I wanted to do it this evening. Here
goes. This is a beautiful stone and an amazing gesture
on your part, for many reasons. By the time I'm through
here, I promise that you'll have your answer....
(She shows the ring off to the audience.) My graduate
advisor gave me this advice five months ago..."Strive to
make art, but change the world." Pretty wise words, I
thought, at the time, and so, being a good little student,
that's what I set out to do. *(She appears almost nervous,
but not quite. She looks at the audience for a moment.)*
With that in mind, I present to you this, my newest
work. It is a *human* sculpture on which I've worked
these past eighteen weeks, and of whom I'm very
proud. I cannot legally name him tonight as he hasn't
yet signed a waiver for the various items on display in
the visual portion, but it's a small college, and a smaller
town, *(Laughs)* so you've got a pretty decent chance at
guessing who it is. In fact, I've done all I could to be as
visible as possible with him this year—I'm more of a
stay-at-home person myself—since I thought that was
an important aspect of his unique transformation. The

piece itself is untitled since I think, I hope, that it will
mean something different to each of you and, frankly,
anyone who sees it. *(She uncovers a large photograph
from a nearby easel. The eyes have been blurred but it is
undeniably the "old"* ADAM.*)* I did the M T V thing here
on the face...this is a "before" picture that I had a
classmate take of us near the Pizza Hut out by the
highway. That was our first official encounter after he
asked me out—at his place of work, a big no-no, or so I
was told—and it was here that I coaxed him into eating
his first vegetarian meal. Well, as vegetarian as a
spinach-and-mushroom calzone can be! He also had
a salad....

*(*JENNY *is suddenly up and storms off toward an exit,
crumpling up her program and throwing it as she goes.*
EVELYN *waits, smiling, then continues.)*

EVELYN: Anyway, he told me that for him, it was a huge
deal and it does mark the beginning of my systematic
makeover, or "sculpting," if you will, of my two very
pliable materials of choice: the human flesh and the
human will. *(Beat)* I first spotted my chosen base
material...it's so funny not to use names! Sorry,
but a lawyer actually told me I had to say that,
"base material"...on January 9th, the fifth day of winter
semester, as I was actively pursuing another set of base
material. Obviously, my current creation appeared
much more right for my work....

(She scans the audience. They are silent, unsure.)

EVELYN: Still with me? You're very quiet...okay. The
exhibit itself will give you many first-hand examples
of my efforts, some hands-on such as video tapes or
sound recordings of our conversations and others more
scientific in nature, as in growth charts, X-rays and
accompanying data. As you can see from this photo,
however, the hair, the glasses, the excessive amount of
weight, offered a number of physical areas that made

him unique and perfect for this project. A short list of
alterations I've induced would include eating better
and losing weight—some twenty-five pounds or more—
an exercise regimen that included both cardiovascular
work and weight training, the purchase of contact
lenses, a complete change in hairstyles and significant
wardrobe alterations as well. He even tattooed his body
for me, without asking...in a highly questionable place.
These are surface items, to be sure, but if I, in fact,
tell you that I'm going through with it and marrying
the guy, you'd probably all shake my hand and say,
"Wow, how the hell can I do that to my boyfriend?"
But this, I'm afraid, was not done out of love or caring
or concern...this was a simple matter of can I instill
"X" amount of change in this creature, using only
manipulation as my palette knife? I made sure that
nothing was ever forced during our sessions or
"sittings" together—I can't really say they were dates,
not on my part, although the allusion of "dating" was
imperative—and that his free will was always at the
forefront of each decision. I made suggestions, created
the illusion of interest and desire, but never said,
"You must do this." Not once. Any questions yet?

(She surveys her audience again. A pin could drop.)

EVELYN: Ummmm...you may be asking yourselves,
"Well, did she at least tell him?" Of course not, no,
I couldn't. Not until tonight, or he really wouldn't be
a piece of art. He would be a jilted lover, a spurned
fiancé, etc. But he is more than that...he's my creation.
Now, it'll be easy for many of you to condemn my
actions as harsh, inhumane or just unrealistic as you
drive or walk home tonight, but how many here can say
that they have never looked at their significant other
and/or a business associate and said, "They're perfect,
they're great, except for just *one* thing..." Well, I too
have taken my base materials and honed them into

something new, something unique and, in the eyes and standards of society, something arguably improved. But, with the artist's ruthless pursuit of truth and historical disregard for rule and law...I've gone a step further. I found that, with the right coaxing of my material—yes, "coaxing" often of a sexual nature, I'll admit—I could hone the inside of my sculpture as well as the surface. I found myself suddenly creating strong moral ambiguity where I could detect only the slightest traces before, often in direct proportion to the amount of external change. This means, as my subject became handsomer and firmer and more confident, his actions became more and more, ahh, *questionable*. Against medical advice, he had work done to his face, cosmetic surgery at age twenty-two, and insisted to those around him that he had merely fallen down. He also started to deceive his friends and myself with greater abandon during this period while showing increased interest in other women. Indeed, he had relations with his best friend's fiancée and continues to harbor details from us about the incident to this day. Moreover, he was willing to give those friends up when asked, walk away from them without any further contact, after said encounter, leading me to an assumption of further wrong-doing with the young woman in question. And, as stated earlier...

(PHILLIP *now stands, walking slowly up an aisle and looking right at* ADAM.)

PHILLIP: ...THIS IS FUCKED.

(*When he is gone,* EVELYN *plows onward.*)

EVELYN: ...these universal corrections culminated in an offer of marriage to me, this coming from a confirmed, albeit young, bachelor. I call this act "morally questionable" because it seems to be motivated, in my mind at least, as much out of guilt as genuine feelings for me. He has then, as I see it, been utterly and totally refashioned as a person. *(Beat)* As my grandfather used to say, "He's a real piece of work..." *(She unveils a large "after" photo for all to see.)* And yet open any fashion magazine, turn on any television program and the world will tell you...he's only gotten more interesting, more desirable, more normal. In a word, *better*. He is a living, breathing example of our obsession with the surface of things, the shape of them. *(Indicating "after" photo)* Not bad, huh? And ladies, he is available. *(To* ADAM*)* This was a startling and unexpected gesture, but obviously, I can't accept.... *(She takes off the ring and places it on an easel.)* You can examine the stone and setting further when it's placed in the exhibit. *(Beat)* As for me, I have no regrets or feelings of remorse for my actions, the manufactured emotions...none of it. I have always stood by the single and simple conceit that I am an artist. Only that. I follow in a long tradition of artists who believe that there is no such concept as religion, or government, community or even family. There is only art. Art that must be created. Whatever the cost.

*(*ADAM *can stand it no longer; he stands and hurries toward the nearest exit. He lets the door SLAM! behind him.)*

EVELYN: Now, you may have a different opinion, *feel* differently, I welcome that. Difference is good. Great. Vital, even. Only indifference is suspect. Only to indifference do I say, "Fuck You".

*(*EVELYN *slowly lifts both middle fingers to her audience, making sure she points them at everyone watching.)*

EVELYN: With that in mind, I present you with my untitled sculpture and supporting materials tonight. Thank you. *(She takes a short bow and steps out of the light.)*

(The exhibition gallery)

(A small studio space painted blood red. Several tables scattered about with various "supporting data" on them.)

*(*EVELYN *standing all alone, punch in one hand, cookie in the other. After a moment, she takes a nibble. She crosses to a box of photos and browses.* ADAM *enters and stares at her.)*

ADAM: ...not a big "modern art" crowd, I guess, huh?

EVELYN: Hey. *(Beat)* Glad you stopped by...

ADAM: Yeah, well, I didn't really have anything to do...plus, I can't show my face in the streets, so it seemed logical.

EVELYN: Look, Adam...

ADAM: Please don't "Look, Adam" me now, okay, or I might not make it through this.... *(Beat)* Just refer to me as "it" or "untitled," it'll help me keep some perspective here.... *(He wanders over and pours some punch. Stuffs a few cookies in his pocket. Shoves three in his mouth and chews them down.)* ...that's gonna shoot some piece of data all to shit, isn't it?

EVELYN: Doesn't matter now, do what you want...you're finished.

ADAM: "You're finished." Wow. *(Considers)* Most people just say, "Hey, sorry, can't marry you." And they say it in private....

EVELYN: ...yeah, that might've been a bit too far.

ADAM: Oh shit, Evelyn, you are so beyond "far" that you're in danger of hitting Uranus. And I mean the planet....

EVELYN: *(Smiling)* See, you're still funny....

ADAM: Just stop, alright? I was never funny, or good-looking or clever. I was nothing until you started dicking around with me. I admit it. No-thing. But you know what? I was absolutely fine with that....

EVELYN: I know this is a lot for you to take in and everything....

ADAM: Uh-huh...I got a little Gregor Samsa thing going right now, so....

EVELYN: I don't get that....

ADAM: Doesn't matter. I do...I get it.

(A moment of dead silence.)

EVELYN: ...listen, I know my work relied on not telling you what was going on, but I....

ADAM: Here in a "small town" we just call it lying....

EVELYN: I did lie to you, yes....

ADAM: Yeah, just a little. *(Beat)* "I'm a very straightforward person..."

EVELYN: I had to say that. Sorry.

ADAM: You're sorry? Well, that's good...I figured I was gonna have to really work to get that one out of you.

EVELYN: *I'm* not sorry. I mean, not for what I've done. I just feel bad that you're so upset....

ADAM: Oh, I see....

EVELYN: I even thought maybe you could handle it. I did, really...otherwise I wouldn't have invited you tonight.

ADAM: Yeah, just me and two hundred of my closest friends.

EVELYN: Adam, you don't have any friends. *(Beat)* You gave up the only ones I've known you to have. Gave 'em up pretty easily...

(ADAM *shivers at this one; she's turned out to be a cool little number.)*

ADAM: Geez...don't hold back at all, please. Call it exactly how you see it.

EVELYN: I just want to keep it as truthful as possible.

ADAM: *(Laughing)* That'll be different....

EVELYN: ...you're so angry....

ADAM: Well, you know, Evelyn, what do you want me to say?! You messed with my life and you put it under fucking glass...that might make anyone a touch cross.

EVELYN: What'd I do wrong? *(Beat)* Seriously, tell me...

ADAM: Screw you...

EVELYN: You have screwed me. A lot. You wanna watch it? There's a cassette over there somewhere.

ADAM: You are seriously fucked up. I mean it....

EVELYN: Yeah...what was so bad? I wanna know, tell me...from your perspective.

ADAM: I'm not gonna give you a last little thrill. Fuck that.

EVELYN: Listen to your mouth, Adam...you never used to talk like that.

ADAM: You're gonna take credit for that, too, huh?

EVELYN: Nope, you picked that up all on your own. Cute guys always have potty mouths. They think it makes 'em cuter....

ADAM: Yeah, well, tell me how "cute" this one is, then...fuck you, you heartless cunt.

EVELYN: So, tell me then. Go ahead, you feel that way about me, you can tell me what I did wrong. *If* I did something wrong....

ADAM: You don't see this as wrong?!

EVELYN: I said, you tell me. I wanna know what you think I did....

(He stops for a moment, taking a deep breath. Not really wanting to engage)

ADAM: You honestly have no concept here....

EVELYN: Just say it....

ADAM: Awww, shit. Look...I don't have time, okay? I'm not gonna stand here....

EVELYN: The exercising? Or was it the new clothes that really bugged you?

ADAM: That is not the....

EVELYN: Everything I did made you a more desirable person, Adam. People began to notice you...take interest in you. I watched them....

ADAM: Well, lucky me. I got to be part of your installation "thingie."

EVELYN: You *are* my installation thingie.... *(Beat)* Look, if you hadn't been here tonight, hadn't heard all this stuff...wouldn't you still be happy? Waiting at home for me, hoping this went well, wanting to make love....

ADAM: That's not the point....

EVELYN: Yes, it is! It's the *total* point. All that stuff we did was real for you, therefore it was real. It wasn't for me, therefore it wasn't. It's all subjective, Adam. Everything.

ADAM: Not love. Not cruelty.

EVELYN: Of course they are....

ADAM: *(Reaching)* I'll tell you something "real,"
I should sue your ass.

EVELYN: You could...I did take that risk.

ADAM: That's right, you did, and you're crazy if you
think I'm gonna let you put all this shit on display. Our
time together. *(Wanders about)* Oh, but you'd love that,
wouldn't you? If I got a lawyer. Then we could fight
this out in public, all the way to the Supreme Court.

EVELYN: Or higher...Jerry Springer. *(Beat)* You should
be proud of this...most of it.

ADAM: Just save it, 'kay? *(Looking about, he spots his old
cord blazer sticking out of a box. Surprised, he pulls it free
and stares at it.)* What's this doing here?

EVELYN: It was only four bucks at the Goodwill....

ADAM: ...why would you buy that?

EVELYN: Just so I'd have it.

ADAM: What?

EVELYN: ...all of you.

*(He scans the room, then throws his hands up. Suddenly,
ADAM pulls off his new coat and tosses it onto the floor.)*

ADAM: ...fine.

EVELYN: What?

ADAM: It's fine, forget it....

EVELYN: What is?

ADAM: What the hell...it can't get any worse. You get
off on showing people my old socks and scuzzy sheets,
go for it....

EVELYN: I don't "get off" on it....

ADAM: My "Fruit of the Looms" mean that much to you, have a field day....

EVELYN: ...Adam, this is my work. *(Beat)* I'll give back whatever you want, soon as I get my grade.

ADAM: Whatever...

EVELYN: I will.

ADAM: The ring'd be nice. It was my grandma's.

EVELYN: I'll take care of it.

ADAM: Thanks. Good...

EVELYN: ...hard feelings?

ADAM: Me? Nah...we had some fun, right?

EVELYN: Yeah.

ADAM: But, hey, that's subjective.

EVELYN: Exactly.

ADAM: Then *I* had some fun, fell in love and all that... and you got yourself a grade and a column inch or two in the school paper. Congrats. Seriously...but do me a favor, don't fool yourself and think that this is "art." 'kay? It's a sick fucking joke, but it is not "art."

EVELYN: Is that right?

ADAM: Pretty much, yeah. *(Beat)* You know, when Picasso took a shit, he didn't call it a "sculpture." He knew the difference. That's what made him *Picasso*. And if I'm wrong about that, I mean, if I totally miss the point here and somehow puking up your own little shitty neuroses all over people's laps *is* actually Art, then you oughta at least realize there's a price to it all...you know? Somebody pays for your two minutes on C N N. Someone always pays for people like you. And if you don't get that, if you can't see at least *that* much...then you're about two inches away from using

babies to make lamp shades and calling it "furniture."
(Beat) I guess I'm done....

EVELYN: Wow. Okay...so, you're saying I should be a
"better person." Is that it?

ADAM: That's the nutshell, yeah.

EVELYN: Better like...*you*?

ADAM: No. Just better... *(Beat)* Anybody can be
provocative, or shocking. Stand up in class and take
a piss, paint yourself blue and run naked through a
church screaming out the names of people you've slept
with. Is that Art, or did you just forget to take your
Ritalin? *(Beat)* It doesn't matter if you call it "Art" if
you have nothing to say. And you don't. *You* just need
attention....

EVELYN: Well, we'll just have to agree to disagree, then,
won't we?

ADAM: Yes, we will. We will definitely do that. *(Beat)*
Don't forget what Oscar Wilde said....

EVELYN: He always had something to say, didn't he?

ADAM: Yeah..."All art is quite useless." He said that.

EVELYN: Huh. I thought you were gonna go with
"Insincerity and treachery somehow seem inseparable
from the artistic temperament." That's a good one, too....

ADAM: It is, yeah. Damn, wish I'd said that.

EVELYN: Don't worry about it...look how he ended up.

ADAM: Yep...alone, penniless and in prison. Everything
I wish for you.... *(Beat)* Tell me, though. One thing.

EVELYN: Yes?

ADAM: Was any of it true?

EVELYN: What do you mean?

ADAM: Not the things we did, or the kind words or whatever...but any of it?

EVELYN: ...no. Not really.

ADAM: I mean about you. The nose-job or Lake Forest or your mother's maiden name. One thing you ever said to me?

EVELYN: My mom's name is Anderson....

ADAM: Oh. Are you twenty-five?

EVELYN: Twenty-two. Just...I skipped two grades.

ADAM: Okay... *(Beat)* And the scars are....

EVELYN: Those were a different project.

ADAM: Got it. I got it...Gemini at least?

EVELYN: No, Pisces. Sorry.

ADAM: Don't be. Hey, it's...*Art.*

EVELYN: ...I should probably get going. I think the Dean wants "a word" with me. *(Ricky Ricardo voice)* "I got some 'splaining to do."

ADAM: What's that from?

EVELYN: Nothing. *I Love Lucy.*

ADAM: Ahh, T V. That other great art form....

EVELYN: Uh-huh. You coming?

ADAM: Nah, not yet... *(Holds up hands)* Don't worry, I'm not gonna do anything to your stuff. No spray paint. I just....

EVELYN: I understand. Go ahead.

ADAM: Thanks...

EVELYN: The door locks if you just close it.

ADAM: Great.

(EVELYN *smiles at him once more, but says nothing.*
What's to say? She heads for the door but stops.)

EVELYN: ...that one time.

ADAM: Huh?

EVELYN: In my bed, one night, when you leaned over
and whispered in my ear...remember?

ADAM: 'Course. I remember everything about us.

EVELYN: And I whispered back to you, I said....

ADAM: I remember.

EVELYN: I meant that. I did.

ADAM: Yeah?

EVELYN: Yes.

ADAM: ...oh.

(*She starts to say something else but catches herself. She goes*
out. ADAM *stands alone in the quiet room, looking about.*)

(*Silence. Darkness*)

END OF PLAY

Neil LaBute

one-act plays licensed by B P P I

A GAGGLE OF SAINTS

ALL APOLOGIES

AUTOBAHN

BENCH SEAT

COAX

FALLING IN LIKE

FUNNY

IPHIGENIAIN OREM

LAND OF THE DEAD

LIARS CLUB

LONG DIVISION

LOVE AT TWENTY

MEDEA REDUX

MERGE

ROAD TRIP

STAND-UP

UNION SQUARE

WRECKS

Neil LaBute

full-length plays licensed by B P P I

THE DISTANCE FROM HERE

FAT PIG

IN A DARK DARK HOUSE

THE MERCY SEAT

THE SHAPE OF THINGS

SOME GIRL(S)

THIS IS HOW IT GOES